TECHNICAL WRITING
An Introduction

Published By
The Yeungnam University Press
2010

214-1, Gyeongsan City, Gyeongsangbuk-do
Tel 053-810-1801～4 Fax 053-810-4722
http://book.yu.ac.kr

First Published
5 March 2010

ISBN 89-7581-291-0 03740

About the Authors

Michael Neil Shapiro
마이클 니을 샤피로

Michael teaches Technical Writing at Yeungnam University's School of Mechanical Engineering, where he has been Associate Foreign Professor for three years. He is a graduate of the University of Toronto and Carleton University, Ottawa, Canada, where he majored in English. He applies practical language skills, to improve the quality of oral and written communication.

In Canada, he taught Business English at Ryerson, in Toronto. At George Brown College, he co-developed a new course in Nurse-Patient Communication. He worked on staff for a number of years at the Canadian National Institute for the Blind, recording "Talking Books" on audio tape.

In Korea, Michael has taught English at Korea University in Seoul, Korea Maritime University, the R.O.K. Naval Academy and Cheju National University. In Seoul, he appeared in a weekly TV-TOEIC series on EBS through BCM. For many years, he has worked as an English editor on projects ranging from magazine & news articles to TOEIC textbooks to government policy papers to academic research and conference proceedings for international publication.

In 2009, he assisted in establishing Engineers Without Borders in Korea.

Sang Woo Joo
주상우

Sang Woo Joo is a professor of Mechanical Engineering, with many published professional articles to his credit. He is Director of the WCU Nano Research Center and Vice President for International Programs at Yeungnam University.

For several years he has promoted publication of a bilingual textbook on Technical Writing and believed that it would be helpful to students in Mechanical Engineering and several other majors.

TECHNICAL WRITING
An Introduction

Michael Neil Shapiro
마이클 니을 샤피로

Sang Woo Joo
주상우

Please advise the publisher in writing
of any errors or omissions, so they may be corrected
in subsequent printings or editions.

서문

새로운 전자제품을 구입하면 사용설명서가 따라옵니다. 어떤 설명서는 제품사용에 많은 도움이 되는 반면 읽을수록 오리무중으로 만드는 것들도 흔히 있습니다. 회사에 새로운 인사제도를 도입하여 설명회를 할 때 어떤 사람은 아주 짧은 시간에 일목요연하게 중요한 내용을 이해하기 쉽도록 얘기해 주지만 어떤 사람은 몇 시간 동안 장황하게 늘어놓아도 뭐가 뭔지 이해하기가 힘든 경우가 있을 것입니다. 꼭 업무만 아니라 일상에서도 상대가 이해하기 쉽게 전화통화나 편지작성을 하는 사람과 그 반대인 사람을 흔히 볼 수 있습니다. 의사소통을 효과적으로 하는 사람과 그렇지 못한 사람의 차이는 무엇일까요? 선천적으로 뛰어난 소통을 하는 사람도 물론 있겠지만 대부분의 매끈한 글이나 발표는 많은 노력과 연습을 통해 나오는 것입니다.

여기서 얘기하는 좋은 글이란 문학적 예술적으로 뛰어난 것을 말하는 것이 아닙니다. Technical writing, 즉 어떠한 특정한 목적을 가지고 쓰는 글에 대한 것을 의미하는 것입니다. 취업을 위해서 작성하는 이력서와 지원서, 예비 고객의 질문에 답하는 e-mail, 환불 신청에 논리적이면서도 예의를 잃지 않는 답변 등 많은 경우를 들 수 있습니다. 단지 과학기술 관련 글만을 얘기하는 것이 아닙니다. 복잡한 현대사회에서 대부분의 사람들은 이제 단순한 감이나 재주로 technical communication을 하지 않습니다. 타당성과 설득력 있게 자신이나 소속 단체에 이익이 되는 글과 말을 전달하는 방법에 대한 과학적인 연구에 과감한 투자를 하고 있습니다. 미국을 선두로 한 선진국에서는 이미 오래전부터 technical communication 또는 rhetorics 전공을 개설하여 박사학위까지 수여해오고 있습니다. 의사전달이 상당한 연구개발을 요하는 기술이라는 것을 단적으로 증명하는 것이라 할 수 있습니다.

국내에서도 최근 의사표현능력의 중요성을 인식하고 많은 관련 교육이 추가 되고 있고 진학 및 입사에 점점 중요하게 반영이 되고 있습니다. 분야와 상관없이 의사소통기술이 성공적인 업무수행에 직결되고 그러한 능력과 업무능력에 상관관계가 있다는 사실은 잘 알려진 결론입니다. 따라서 우리는 주어진 시간과 공간에 정확하고 효과적으로 필요한 뜻을 전달하는 훈련을 쌓아 나가야 합니다.

그런 의미에서 이 책은 영어를 배우기 위해 쓰여진 것이 아닙니다. 단순히 영문 문서작성의 format을 주지시키기 위해 정리된 것도 아닙니다. 그렇다고 효과적인 의사소통을 위한 방법론에 대해 설명하는 것도 아닙니다. 영문으로 현재 통용되고 있는 technical communication을 그 형태별로 알아보면서 독자 또는 시청자를 겨냥하여 정확한 의사 전달의 목적을 달성할 수 있는 내용구성을 위한 훈련을 가장 중요한 목표로 삼았습니다. 이 책을 읽으면서 물론 영어실력의 향상도 따르겠지만 이러한 것은 부수적이라는 것을 독자들께서 이해해주시기 바랍니다. 아주 깊은 연구가 되어 있는 의사소통 이론에 관한 내용은 다년간 영어의사소통기술(Technical Communication in English)란 3학점 대학과목으로 강의하기 때문에 여기서는 취급하지 않고 실례를 통해 알기 쉽게 전달되도록 하는 부분에 노력을 집중하였습니다.

대부분의 내용은 번역 또는 혼용 없이 영어 그대로 적혀있습니다. 독자들에게 도움이 될 몇몇 부분만 한글로 표현이 되어 있습니다. 이 책이 장차 독자들의 영어 의사전달 기술 향상에 조금이나마 기여가 되기를 기대합니다. 항상 상대(audience)를 목표로 하여 소통내용의 밀도(information density)를 고려하는 전문인이 되기를 바라겠습니다.

2010년 2월 주상우

ACKNOWLEDGEMENTS, Bilingual Edition

I'd like to thank the following people for contributing to this textbook and supporting this Technical Writing course:

Prof. Lee, Jeh Won, Director of Finance, Yeungnam University, Republic of Korea and former Chairman (2007-8), School of Mechanical Engineering, for his warm welcome.
Prof. Han, Yongoun, Chairman (2009 - 2010), School of Mechanical Engineering, for consistently and thoughtfully facilitating and encouraging my efforts.
Prof. Lee, Byeong Wan, Director, YU FLI (2009 -) for appointing able colleagues to teach this course, and for expressing his opinion of limiting class size to 25 students.
Prof. Joo, Sang Woo, President of International Affairs (2009 -), Prof. of Mech. Eng., for suggesting a bilingual (English-Korean) textbook, and for hiring me in the first place.
Prof. Sah, Jongyoub for providing the USB memory stick, and further practical help.
Prof. Chung, Mo for many contributions and for his work in founding and funding the first-and-only chapter of Engineers Without Borders - Korea, established June 2009.

Translations into Korean

Prof. Park, Sang Shin, for translating my essay, "Writing Is A Technology," into Korean.
Prof. Yun, Suk-im, for proofreading the Korean version of "Writing Is A Technology".
Prof. Lee, Won Kyoung, for translating "How to read a scientific article". Critically.
Prof. Shim, Jaesool and Alice Mira Chung, for "How To Write A Business Letter".
Ms. Alice Mira Chung, for "Engineering Low-Tech Solutions for Places in Need".
Mr. Dae-hyung Shon for his substantial contributions throughout the text.
Mrs. Won Hee Kim for her very helpful contributions at a busy time.
Prof. Chung, Mo for proofreading and "streamlining" many translations, and for defining Technical Writing and Good Technical Writing in Korean, as we use these terms in this course.

More thanks to

My new teaching colleagues, for bravely taking on respective sections of this course.

The capable staff of the Mechanical Engineering Administrative Office, for helping me navigate YNU's "Easy" computer system and for arranging exams and so many things.

My Korean and International students who, in their hundreds and in their variety, have taught me as much about the process of learning to write as I have ever taught them.

Special thanks to Isabelle Nguyen for "Européen[n]e" and **Ni Chen** for the word "follow" in the Description of Good Technical Writing.

Yeungnam University for providing the opportunity to develop, present and refine this course and this textbook.

MNS
Gyeongsan-si, R.O.K.
December 2009

PREFACE to BILINGUAL Edition 2010

Technical Writing, An Introduction provides materials for a one-semester course. It was originally designed and refined primarily for 3rd year Mechanical Engineering students in Korea.

However, a motivated individual, working alone, could learn the principles, do the exercises and produce technically correct writing in English. The sincere student of writing can progress from writing a sentence in active form and inserting proper punctuation, to avoiding intellectual theft—plagiarism—by citing their sources of information and simply giving credit where it is due.

A more advanced textbook, "Term Two", would apply the same methods and principles, but it would offer longer, more challenging exercises and explore a greater variety of applications.

This BILINGUAL edition offers the reader three (3) clear benefits:

- **Many items, especially "How To" articles, are now translated into Korean.**
- **Short forms (acronyms) are used frequently, to make key ideas memorable.**
- **Readability statistics—classic technical writing tools—are simply explained.**

In this edition, "C.A.R. Statistics" move from the lecture room into pages of print. This term is at once a concept, an acronym and a mnemonic device. My purpose is to drive home, with a smile, how these Readability scores can help every writer to produce better finished writing.

These added benefits cost something: for a writer, a translator or an editor, they cost time and effort, thought and imagination. I heartily thank all contributors listed in the Acknowledgements. For the reader, the book is also demanding. It has more pages. It weighs a little more and it costs a little more. Good value at twice the price.

In "Pedagogically Speaking," I've added Day One resources & commentary for the teacher.

Revising a textbook is Continuous Quality Improvement (CQI) in action. A bow to ABEEK. Working hard to make ideas clear and memorable in writing can also be great fun! I've long thought it was important to have some fun—serious fun—with my students. This is especially true with my Engineering students, since writing and English are not necessarily their favorite subjects. Math is not mine. For many engineers, the word-equation is:

Writing + English = Headache!

I hope this edition brings the spirit of "serious fun" into the written presentation. It also includes some tough and detailed criticism of professional writing & students' assignments as submitted.

The new TOEIC test, as you may know, now includes a writing section. This course may also help students with that test. There's a lot to be said about TOEIC, not all of it favorable. I share some wry thoughts on **T.O.E.I.C.** in the **Teacher's Manual.** For now, here are three: **T.O.E.I.C.**

Teach Only Essential, Important Concepts.

Thoughtful Organization Evokes Intelligent Composition.

Tension Over English Instruction Continues.

This may be the first bilingual (English/Korean) textbook on Technical Writing to be published in Korea. If that is true, I'm pleased to be a pioneer.

I wish all my students, colleagues and readers great success!

Statistics (V-21): Words 484; s/p 2.0, w/s 12.1; passive sent. 10% Reading ease 50.1, Grade level 9.2

Michael Neil Shapiro
Gyeongsan-si, R.O.K. 2009.12.21

2010 년 이중언어 판 서문

Technical Writing, An Introduction 은 한 학기 분량의 교재이다. 본 교재는 원래 한국의 3 학년 기계공학과 학생들을 위해 설계되고 다듬어졌다.

그러나 글쓰기에 흥미를 가진 사람은 혼자서라도 기본 원칙을 배우고 작문연습을 해서 올바른 영작문을 할 수 있다. 글쓰기에 성실한 학생은 능동형 문장 작성에서부터 구두법 삽입, 그리고 인용된 정보를 표시하고, 저작권을 인정함으로써 지적재산권 침해—표절을 피하는 방법까지 배우게 될 것이다.

더욱 심화된 교재인 "Term Two" 역시 같은 방법과 원칙을 적용하였지만 한층 더 길고 어려운 문제를 제시하고, 더욱 많은 양의 다양한 사례들을 다루게 될 것이다.

이번 이중언어 판은 독자들에게 3 가지 명확한 이점을 제공한다:

- 많은 부분, 특히 "How To" 부분들이 한국어로 번역되었다.
- 중요한 개념들을 기억하기 쉽게 하기 위해 단어 첫 글자만 이용한 줄임말이 사용되었다.
- 분장난이도 통계치(readability statistics)-지금은 의사소통 글쓰기에 있어 표준 분석 도구가 된-에 대해 간결하게 설명되어 있다.

이 개정판에서는, "C.A.R. Statistics"가 강의실에서만 보여주다가 활자판으로 옮겨졌다. 이것은 한 때는 기억하기 쉽게 하기 위한 도구이자 줄임말 정도의 개념이었다. 이 문장난이도 점수(readability score) 체계가 독자들이 더 좋은 작문을 하는데 많은 도움을 줄 수 있다면 더 이상 바랄 것이 없겠다.

이 개정판에 보강된 부분들을 수고하신 분들이 있다. 작가, 번역가, 편집자가 그 분들이다. 이분들은 이 교재를 위해 시간과 노력, 그리고 갖고 계신 생각과 상상력을 아끼지 않았다. 그리고 감사의 글에서 언급했던 도움을 주신 모든 분들께 진심으로 감사 드린다. 이 책이 독자에게 요구하는 것 또한 많아졌다. 책 분량이 늘었고, 책 무게도 좀 늘었으며, 책 값도 다소 인상되었다. 그러나 책 값의 2 배 이상의 가치가 있을 것이다.

교수법적인 측면에서, 선생님들을 위해 "Day One resources & commentary"를 추가하였다.

교과서를 개정한다는 것은 지속적으로 질을 향상시키는 것이다. ABEEK 에 경의를 표한다.
자신의 생각들을 명확하고 인상적일 수 있도록 글로 남기는 작업은 아주 재미있는 일이 될 수 있다! 나는 학생들과 함께 재미-진정한 재미-를 느끼는 것이 매우 중요하다고 오래 전부터 생각해 왔다. 이것은 특히 기계공학부 학생들과 같은 이공계 학생들에게 있어 맞는 말이다. 왜냐하면 내가 수학을 좋아하지 않듯이 글쓰기와 영어가 그 학생들이 가장 좋아하는 과목은 아니기 때문이다. 많은 엔지니어들에 문자방정식은 다음과 같다

글쓰기+ 영어 = 골치거리!

이번 개정판을 통해 글쓰기를 통한 의사표현에 "진정한 재미"를 붙일 수 있기를 바란다. 이 개정판은 또한 전문적인 글과 학생들이 제출한 과제물에 대한 냉정하고 상세한 비판을 포함한다.

새로운 TOEIC 시험에 글쓰기가 포함된다는 것을 알고 있을 것이다. 이 교재는 토익시험을 준비하는 학생들에게도 도움이 될수 있을 것이다. 토익시험에 대해 의견이 분분한데 모두 호의적인 의견만 있는 것은 아니다. 강사를 위한 매뉴얼에서 토익대해 쓴 소리를 좀 하고자 한다. 여기서는 다만 세가지만 언급하고자 한다. T.O.E.I.C.은,

Teach Only Essential, Important Concepts.
본질적이고 중요한 개념만 가르쳐라.

Thoughtful Organization Evokes Intelligent Composition.
사려 깊은 글 구성이 훌륭한 글쓰기를 이끌어낸다.

Tension Over English Instruction Continues.
영어 교습에 대한 긴장은 계속된다.

이 개정판이 한국에서 처음으로 출판되는 영한 이중언어 이공계 학생용 영작문 교재일 수도 있기에 이 분야의 새로운 개척자가 될 수 있음을 자랑스럽게 생각한다.

학생들과 동료들 그리고 독자 여러분의 성공을 기원한다.

Michael Neil Shapiro
대한민국 경산. *2009.11.24*

머리말과 감사의 글

2 판, 08 봄

이 Course Notes 는 내가 지금껏 글쓰기에 관해 배워온 것과 가르친 것들을 들고 다니기 쉽도록 책으로 정리한 것이다. 이 책은 내가 예전부터 있었으면 좋겠다고 생각해온 그런 책이기도 하다. 이 Course Notes 는 교과서이자 가이드북, 연습장이라 할 수 있고 많은 예제와 참고용 자료들이 포함되어 있다.

글쓰기란 끝이 없는 일련의 개선 과정이다. 일 년 내에 배울 수 있는 것도 아니거니와 한 시간 만에 작업을 끝낼 수 있는 것도 아니다. 어떤 이들은 글을 쓴다는 것은 "마음에 들 때까지 계속해서 다시 쓰는 것이다" 라고 한다. 어떤 사람은 다른 성공과 마찬가지로 10%의 영감과 90%의 노력이라고도 한다.
글쓰기의 성취는 우리의 정열, 관심, 지능, 지식, 기술 그리고 가용 시간 등에 의해 항상 제한되게 마련이다. 나는 이 책을 만드는데 내 모든 역량을 다해 최선을 다해 노력해보았다.

나를 앞서 지도해 주신 은사님들, 도움과 자문을 아끼지 않은 동료들에게 감사드리며, 특히 이 책에서 언급된 몇몇 분들에게 감사 드린다. 특별히 이 프로젝트에 대해 유난히 수고하신 분들이 계신다.

책자표지의 한글 문장과 훈민정음의 이미지를 제공 해주신 정모 교수님과, 이웃이자 많은 도움과 자문을 주셨고 의사소통 기술에서 디자인의 중요성을 알려주셨던 이원경 교수님께 감사 드린다. 이 교수님은 유머감각도 대단하셔서 한번은 내가 학생에게 BC 의 뜻은 Before Computer 라고 했더니 이 교수님은 그럼 "AD 는 After Digital 되어야겠네."라고 했다. 이런 연유로 해서 본 일화는 이 책의 한 장(章)의 제목이 되기도 했다.

고려대학교에 재직 중이신 피터 실베스터 교수님은 핵심을 찌르는 글 솜씨와 더불어 아직도 대학생 같은 학구적 정신을 소유하고 계시다. 선생님의 혹독한 비평과 조언 그리고 오랜 기간 함께 나눠온 우정에 감사한다.

그리고, 여기에 미처 언급하지 못한 다른 많은 분들의 든든한 지지와 우정에도 감사 드린다.

그리고 마지막으로 항상 나를 보살펴주고, 지지해주고, 나의 가장 중요한 일부이면서 날카로운 비평감각을 가졌고 여행계획까지 세워주며 매일 따뜻한 사랑을 보내주는 아내 Eva 에게 고마움을 전한다.

Michael Neil Shapiro
대한민국 경산에서

(Mini Rev.) 2008.8

FOREWORD & ACKNOWLEDGEMENTS

Second Edition, Spring 2008

These ***Course Notes*** gather in one portable package much of what I have learned about writing, and the teaching of writing. It's the kind of "book" that I wish I had had years ago.

Course Notes is a textbook, a guide, a workbook, a collection of writing samples and a reference manual.

Writing is a process. It is not learned in a year. It is not completed in an hour. Some say writing is re-writing. Some say it is—like other achievements—10% inspiration, 90% perspiration.

Our achievements are always limited, by our energy, interest, intellect, knowledge, technique and the available time. I've tried to make the best of mine.

I am grateful for the guidance of teachers who have preceded me, especially the few cited. I am grateful for the assistance and consultation many colleagues have provided. For this project, I must mention specifically:

Professor Chung Mo, who provided the Hangeul sentence for the front cover, and images of *Hūnminjeongeum.*

Professor Lee Won-Kyoung, my neighbour, for help and consultation on many issues and occasions, and for insisting on the importance of **design** in technical writing. I especially appreciate this humour: When I said that, to our students, B.C. now means Before Computers, he replied: "Then, A.D. must mean After Digital." Hence, the chapter headings.

Professor Peter Sylvestre, of Korea University, for his pithy essays, but more broadly, for the collegial spirit, wry commentary, advice and friendship we've shared over the years.

I am glad of the support and friendship of many others, not here mentioned.

Finally, I am grateful for the care, support, essential organization, critical insights, travel planning and daily affection of my wife, Eva.

Michael Neil Shapiro
Gyeongsan, South Korea

(Mini Rev.) 2008.8

"An education that does not teach clear, coherent writing
cannot provide our world with thoughtful adults;
it gives us instead, at the best, clever children of all ages."

Richard Mitchell, ***Less Than Words Can Say***, Chapter 3.

"Writing," he says, "kept me alive. I sometimes thought about a letter for a week before writing anything. It's something that you must do even if you do not have the leisure of being in prison. To write, you must work methodically, forming your thoughts and prompting other people to think as they read. Writing requires work at both ends. That's what makes it special."

Wei Jingsheng Quoted in "**The Power of Writing**"

By Joel L. Swerdlow. ***National Geographic***, August 1999

"Vigorous[1] writing is concise[2]. A sentence should contain no unnecessary words, a paragraph no unnecessary sentences, for the same reason that a drawing should have no unnecessary lines and a machine no unnecessary parts."

*(Wm. Strunk, Jr., **Elements of Style**, 1918)*

1. vigorous = strong, active, energetic 2. concise = brief and clear

TABLE OF CONTENTS

PART 6 E-MAIL JOB APPLICATIONS

Send An Effective E-mail

Teaching Point: Send a correct and effective e-mail.

PART 7 IMPROVE YOUR JOB APPLICATION LETTER

Teaching Point: Design Your Own Job Application Package

★ Graded Assignment – CLR & Resume 20% ★

PART 8 WRITING A GENERAL BUSINESS OR SALES LETTER

PART 9 TWO RADIO SCRIPTS FROM V.O.A. SPECIAL ENGLISH

PART 1 - ORIENTATION

Course Description & Academic Goal

Of Course! Some Early And Obvious Advice

۞ A 학점을 받는 요령

Hints Toward Getting An 'A'

۞ 이 과목은 어떻게 진행되는가

How This Course Works

Attendance Messages in English

۞ 성공적으로 의사소통을 하는 작가, 성공하는 학생

The Successful Technical Writer; The Successful Student

SMS Text Messaging, Essay

SMS Short Forms in English for Messages & Chat

Limit Your Worries

Technical Writing–Toward a Definition

Three Key Words Defined

Technical Writing - A Working Definition in Plain English

Good Technical Writing - A Description

► D.I.Y. Exercise: Write the same ideas in your own language

TECHNICAL WRITING

Course Description & Academic Goal

Custom Designs for Effective Communication

Almost everyone recognizes the established forms of written communication: advertisement, business letter, e-mail, job application, news release, owner's manual, questionnaire, resumé & journal article or scientific report.

We know them at a glance.

We can use and shape these standard forms to complete each new task in professional, written communication.

The academic goal of this course is to produce effective writing by conscious design.

▲
▲▲

Readability Statistics:
Words 74, Sentences 4
Sentences per Para. 1.0
Words per Sentence 10.0
Passive Sentences 0%
Flesch Reading Ease 50.7
Grade Level 8.6

■■■■■

Michael Neil Shapiro *August 2009 (V-30)*

CD & AG *Technical Writing, An Introduction* *2009.12 © mns*

OF COURSE!

Some Early And Obvious Advice:

☺ ☻ ☺

How to Win

Come to Class.

Buy the Book.

Do the Work.

†

How to Lose

Don't Attend.

Avoid Assignments.

Skip Exams.

†

Rest In Peace

It's up to you. It's down to you.

You can produce results or excuses.

필승!

Statistics: Words 45; s/p 1.1, w/s 3.1; passives 0%, Reading Ease 94.5, Grade Level 0.8

How to Win or Lose (V-8) *Technical Writing, An Introduction* *2009.8 © Michael N. Shapiro*

A 학점을 받는 요령

이 페이지를 다 읽고 나면 A 학점을 받을 수 있을까? 정답은 요령만 익힌다면 YES 이다.

학기 전반기에 해야 할 가장 중요한 것들은 다음과 같다.

MS 워드 프로그램에 철자 및 문법 체크 기능을 켜라
문장난이도에 관한 통계자료 확인 기능을 활성화하고 무엇을 의미하는지 배워라
이러한 기술적 도구들을 취업지원서 제출 전에 사용하라.

학기 후반기에 해야 할 가장 중요한 것들은 다음과 같다.

수업시간에 각 매뉴얼과 경험의 법칙[1]에 대한 연습문제를 푼다.
두 매뉴얼의 복습 문제를 다 푼 후 "검토" 도구를 적용하고 새로 만들어진 문장난이도 통계자료를 과제에 포함한다.

요약해 정리하면:

학점: 학생들은 2 편의 글쓰기 과제물을 제출해야 한다.

시간 제한: 과제물은 정시에 제출해야 하고, 늦는 경우에는 원래 학점의 반을 잃는다.

시험: 중간고사와 기말고사. 상세한 것은 추후에 공지할 것이다.

교과서를 공부하고, 출석을 잘하고, 숙제를 열심히 하라. 그러면 반드시 좋은 학점을 얻게 될 것이다. 필승!

출석: 출석하는 것은 학생의 책무다. 여러분은 성인이다. ID 만들어서 집에 두지 말고 매일 들고다녀라. 결석할 때마다 결석을 할때마다 출석시스템에 영어로 사유를 간결하고 짤막하게 적어서 제출하라. 그래야 기록을 수정할 수 있다. 내가 도와줄 수 있는 상황이라면 도와주도록 하겠다. (출석관련 메시지를 참고하라)

(Rev. 30) 문장난이도 통계치: 단어 185; 단락당 문장 수 1.9, 문장당 단어 수 8.3; 문장난이도: 수동태 0%, 난이도 단계 95.6, 수준 2.2

Hints for getting an 'A' *Technical Writing, An Introduction* *2009.11.29 © Mns*

[1] 경험의 법칙, Rules of Thumb, 과거 경험을 토대로 항상 맞진 않지만 나름 적용하는 법칙

HINTS TOWARD GETTING AN 'A'

Can I get an 'A' in this course by reading this page? Yes, if you can take a hint!

The most important things you can do in the first half of the semester are:

Turn on the Spelling and Grammar Check Tools in Microsoft Word.
Enable the Readability Statistics and learn what they mean.
Apply these technical tools to your job application letter before you hand it in.

The most important things you can do in the second half of the semester are:

Complete in class the exercises on each Manual and on Rules of Thumb.
Complete the Review Assignment on the two Manuals. Apply the "proofing" tools and add your new statistics before you hand in your work for a grade.

Brass tacks:

Grading: I will require at least two (2) written assignments for detailed marking & grading.

Time limits: Do submit assignments on time. Late assignments will lose half their value.

Exams: There will be a mid-term exam and a final exam. Details to be announced: (TBA).

Study the textbook. Attend the lectures. Do the work. Earn the grades. *Pil sung!*

Attendance: Attending class is your responsibility. You are an adult. Get an I.D. card. Carry the card. Use it every day. Don't leave it at home. For each **absence**, write me a short, clear note, in English, on the attendance system (출석시스템), so I can adjust your record. I will help you when I can. (See ***Attendance Messages***.)

(Rev. 30) Statistics: words 223; s/p 2.6, w/s 7.0; Readability: passives 3%, reading ease 79.4, grade level 3.9

이 과목은 어떻게 진행되는가

이 과목은 영어로 글을 잘 쓰는 방법 또는 더 잘 쓰는 방법을 한 한기 동안 배우는 **실용적인 과목이다**.

학기 전반기에는 의사소통에 적합한 글쓰기란 어떤 것 인지 그것에 대한 개관을 훑어본다. 즉, 능동태를 쓰는 좋은 문장들을 쓰는 것과 표준화된 스타일로 문단을 구분하는 방법들을 다룰 것이다. 학생들은 엑셀 프로그램을 이용하여 이력서를 만들고, MS-Word 를 이용하여 철자와 문법 체크를 하는 기능을 배울 것이다. 그리고 문장난이도 체크 기능도 사용할 수 있을 것이다. 나는 이것을 "CAR Statistics" 라고 부른다. 학생들은 이런 기술적인 도구들을 사용함으로써 더욱 좋은 글을 쓸 수 있고 좋은 학점을 받는데 큰 도움이 될 것이다. **MS-Word 가 이 과정의 표준 워드프로로 사용될 것이다.**

우리는 기계공학 리포트에 나오는 긴 문장들을 새롭게 고쳐 써볼 것이다. 그리고 새로운 기술적인 도구들을 사용하여 학생 자신의 입사지원서를 써볼 것이다. 이 입사지원서 또는 커버레터("cover" letter)는 잠재적 고용주에게 학생 자신과 학생의 이력에 대한 소개를 포함한다. 커버레터의 기본 형식은 이메일이나 서면 이력서에도 유용하게 쓸 수 있다. 이 과정의 전반기는 입사에 필요한 기술들은 효과적으로 향상시키고 그리고 불필요하고 소모적인 실수들을 없애는 데 도움이 될 것이다.

학기 후반기에는 사람들이 가정에서 흔하게 보는 두 전기제품의 사용설명서를 살펴볼 것이다. 우리는 설명서의 전체적인 구성과 내용을 고려하고 이 설명서의 어떤 점이 독자들에게 유용한지에 대해 토론을 할 것이다. 그리고 일반적으로 통용되는 법칙을 간략하게 읽고 한두 가지 정도 스케치해보면서 실제로 어느 정도 이 법칙들을 이해했는지 체크해볼 것이다. 또한 과학논문들을 비평적으로 읽는 방법에 대한 조언도 얻을 수 있을 것이다. 우리는 의학연구리포트의 한 부분을 대중들도 읽고 이해하기 쉽도록 새로 고쳐 써볼 것이다. 그리고 적절한 때, 시험 잘 치는 요령또한 배울 것이다. 마지막으로 학생들이 성공으로 가는 열쇠를 찾기를 희망한다.

이 과정은 실용성을 추구한다. 듣기도 아니고, 말하기, 읽기, 그냥 관찰하는 과목은 더욱 아니다. 우리는 수업시간에 꽤 많은 짧막한 글쓰기 연습을 해 볼 것이다. 나는 학생들이 이 글쓰기 연습들을 성실히 해주기를 바란다. 글을 잘 쓰기 위해서는 시간과 연습, 노력 그리고 관심이 필요하다.

나의 좌우명[1]중 하나는"당신은 일에 대한 결과를 만들어 내든지 아니면 그것에 대한 변명을 만들 수 있어야 한다. 알아서 결정해라"이다.

(V-32) 문장난이도 통계치: 단어 309; 단락당 문장 수 4.5, 문장당 단어 수 11.2; 문장난이도: 수동태 0%, 난이도 단계 86, 수준 4

How this course works *Technical Writing, An Introduction* *2009.11.17 © Mns*

[1] **좌우명**, 명사, 정의 2. 삶의 가르침으로 삼는 짧은 표현, Merriam-Webster 온라인 사전, www.m-w.com

How This Course Works

This is a practical, one-semester course in how to write well, or much better, in English.

In the first half of the semester, we review Technically Correct Writing. We'll make good sentences in active form and separate paragraphs in a standard style. On your computer, you'll complete an ***Excel*** Resume form. In ***MS-Word,*** you'll activate the Spelling and Grammar Check Tools. Then, you'll enable Readability Statistics. I call them "C.A.R. Statistics". You'll learn to use these technical tools to help yourself become a better writer and get a better grade. Note that **Microsoft Word is the standard word-processing program for this course.**

We'll re-write a long sentence from a Mechanical Engineering Report. You'll apply the technical tools to creating your own Job Application Letter. This JAL or "Cover" letter will introduce you and your Resumé to potential employers. In its basic form, it's useful for both e-mail and paper applications. This early part of the course will help you to promote your job-related skills effectively, and avoid some costly, needless mistakes.

In the second half of the semester, we examine Instruction manuals for two electrical products that people commonly use at home. We'll consider the organization and content of these handbooks, and discuss what features make a manual useful to a reader. Then, we'll read some Rules of Thumb aloud and check your practical understanding by sketching one or two. You'll receive advice on how to read a scientific paper critically. We'll improve part of a medical research report so a normal human can read and understand it. Just in time, you'll get tips for taking exams. I hope, at the end, you'll find the Keys to the Kingdom.

This is a practical course. It's not just listening, speaking, reading or observing. We'll do a good number of short, written exercises, usually in class. I encourage you to put sincere effort into these class exercises. Writing well does take time and work, effort and attention.

One of my mottos[1] is: "You can produce RESULTS or EXCUSES. Decide."

(V-33) Statistics: words 341; s/p 4.6, w/s 12.0; Readability: passives 0%, reading ease 61.8, grade level 7.6

How this course works *Technical Writing, An Introduction* *2009.11.17 © Mns*

[1]**Motto,** *noun. Def'n 2. a short expression of a guiding principle. Merriam-Webster Online Dictionary, www.m-w.com/*

ATTENDANCE MESSAGES

(Useful Sentences, Written in English)

This is a course in English communication in writing.

1. As you know, **your attendance is required** for all classes.
2. However, sometimes it is not possible for you to attend.
3. When you miss class, or can't check in, you must send me a message—in English—on the attendance system. If your explanation seems reasonable, I may, on occasion, excuse your absence on the system.
4. Of course, I appreciate your <u>telling me, in person</u>, that there's a problem. Then I know to look for your written message.

5. Here are some simple sentences you can use to communicate with me.

Listen, and say them out loud:

▶ Sorry, I don't have my attendance card yet.
▶ Sorry, I forgot my card at home. <u>*Or*</u>,
▶ No card today. Sorry. (***ONE TIME*** per semester I may help you with this.)
▶ Sorry, I was late. (I will <u>mark</u> you "late". It's an available "middle" option.)

6. Here are some more simple, sample sentences. Listen, and say:

▶ On Monday, I had a job interview.
▶ On Tuesday, I attended a conference.
▶ On Wednesday, I had military reserve duty. (Or, "Army duty")
▶ On Thursday afternoon, I had a dentist appointment.
▶ On Friday, my brother got married.

Wow! What a busy week!

Statistics(V-11): Words 207 sentences/para. 1.7, words/sentence 7.7; passives 0%, Reading Ease 74.0, Grade Level 4.8

성공적으로 의사소통을 하는 작가

"성공적으로 의사소통을 하는 작가는 독자들과
가장 성공적인 의사소통을 위해 각 페이지를 설계한다."

MNS

성공하는 학생

글쓰기 수업에서 성공하는 학생들은 다음과 같은 행동을 한다.

1. 영어로 쓰여진 **지시사항을** 자세히 읽고 그대로 따라 한다.
2. 각 문장의 처음과 끝을 명확히 표시한다.
3. 능동적이고, 활력적인 문장을 위해 **능동형** 동사를 쓴다.
4. 문단 구분을 확실히 하고, 표준화된 방법을 사용한다.
5. 모든 과제물이나 시험에는 A4 용지, 흑색 (또는 어두운) 펜을 사용하는 등 표준화 된 것을 사용한다.
6. 워드프로세서에서 선생님이 정한 페이지의 여백 규격과 글씨체를 사용한다.
7. 의사소통 목적에 맞는 글쓰기를 위해 철자체크와 문장난이도 체크 기능을 사용한다.
8. 같은 수업을 듣는 동료들의 글을 교정하고, 편집하는데 도움을 준다.
9. 과제물은 정시에 제출하고 글쓴이가 누군지 확실히 표시한다.
10. 수업시간에 배운 지식을 자신의 글쓰기 습관에 반영한다.

문장난이도 통계치

문장난이도 통계치: 단어 114; 단락당 문장 수 1.0, 문장당 단어 수 7.9; 수동태 0%, 난이도 단계 82.1, 수준 3.7

THE SUCCESSFUL TECHNICAL WRITER

"The successful technical writer designs each page for maximum communication with the reader."

MNS

THE SUCCESSFUL STUDENT

The successful student in this writing course will:

1. Read and follow INSTRUCTIONS, written in English.
2. Clearly mark the beginning and end of each sentence.
3. Use *ACTIVE* verbs to make active, energetic sentences.
4. Make paragraph divisions obvious, using a standard method.
5. Use standard, A4 paper and black (or dark) INK on all assignments and exams.
6. Set margins and fonts, acceptable to the course instructor, on Microsoft Word.
7. Use Spell Check and Readability statistics to produce technically correct writing.
8. Help classmates by carefully proofreading and editing their partner's work.
9. Hand in assignments on time, and fully identify himself/herself as the writer.
10. Turn the knowledge presented in this course into excellent writing HABITS.

Readability Statistics

Statistics: Words 132; s/p 1.0, w /sentence 9.9; passives 0%, Reading Ease 48.5, Grade Level 8.9

Successful TW (V-16) *Technical Writing, An Introduction* *2009.8 (2008) © mns*

SMS TEXT MESSAGING

Today, no textbook on "Technical Writing" would be complete without a nod to the "new" and "ubiquitous" technology of text messaging.

A text message is also called an SMS message. SMS means Short Message Service.

Text messaging means composing brief messages using a very limited number of characters or alphabetical letters and sending them to another person.

Usually, each person uses a mobile phone.

Sending text messages is much less expensive than having a voice conversation on the same mobile phone. And it imposes the technical demand that the messages must be short. My university's short message service for teachers has a limit of seventy (70) characters per message. Messages can be saved, re-read, replied to or deleted. They are delivered almost instantly, or as soon as the receiving device joins the network.

We can compose and send text messages from an office or personal computer. This can provide great efficiencies. For example, I can compose a single message and send it at once to all 50 students in my class. I just check a box that means "send to all", and click "send". Using SMS, I can quickly notify all my students of any change in a class meeting time or location.

Or I can send a message to a single student about an individual concern.

SMS messages and their host devices are a relatively "new" technology. They are "ubiquitous" because almost everyone has one.

But there's a big danger. People distracted by text messaging while driving are extremely dangerous—to themselves and to other members of the travelling public.

"Motorists who send text messages while driving are "significantly more impaired" than those who drive drunk, even at the minimum legal limit for alcohol, according to a British study....

"When texting, drivers are distracted by taking their hand off the wheel to use their phone, by trying to read small text on the phone display, and by thinking about how to write their message," said [chief researcher]Reed.

"The study comes on the heels of reports that texting was to blame when a commuter train slammed head-on into a freight train in Los Angles two weeks ago, killing 25 people.

"Officials believe the engineer on the commuter train was texting at the time. Los Angeles-area officials reacted this week by banning the use of all mobile devices by anyone at the controls of a moving train."*

So, enjoy SMS messaging, but stay safe!

Statistics: Words 407; s/p 2.0, w/s 15.5; passives 11%, Reading Ease 58.0, Grade Level 9.0

* *http://www.cbc.ca/consumer/story/2008/09/22/texting-driving.html*

SMS Text Messaging (V-6) *Technical Writing, An Introduction* *2009.9 © Michael Shapiro*

SMS Short Forms in English for Messages & Chat

ASAP	As Soon As Possible
B4	Before
BBL	Be Back Later
BRB	Be Right Back
CU	See You
CUZ	Because
FAQ	Frequently Asked Questions
FYI	For Your Information
IDK	I Don't Know
IOU	I Owe You
J/K	Just Kidding
K	OK
L8R	Later
M/F	Male/Female
MSG	Message
OIC	Oh, I See
OMG!	Oh, My God!
PLZ	Please
SYL	See You Later
TGIF	Thank Goodness It's Friday
THX	Thanks
TTYL	Talk To You Later

Statistics: Words 84; Reading Ease 100%

SMS & Chat (V-5) *Technical Writing, An Introduction* *2009.9, mns*

LIMIT YOUR WORRIES

Speaking and writing can be challenging!

Speaking and writing in a foreign language, or even in our own, can be challenging!

For example, we often worry about choosing the right word (vocab.) and word relationships (grammar) to say what we mean. This is true in both writing and speaking.

But writing is also different from speaking. Each has its advantages and its problems.

The good news is, we need not worry about EVERYTHING at the same time!

LIMIT YOUR WORRIES!

In speaking, we often worry about pronunciation, accent and speed.

In writing, we need not worry about those things.

In writing, we often worry about spelling, punctuation and paragraphs.

In speaking, we need not worry about those things.

In short:

- **When you speak, you need not worry about spelling.**
- **And when you write, you need not worry about pronunciation.**

So, limit your worries. Reduce your stress!

THINK ABOUT THE OTHER GUY, TOO.

It's natural to worry about yourself, first. Am I doing things correctly? Did I say it right?

But then, we need to think about the person who receives the message. Can that person understand my message? Do they get it? How can I help them understand me?

Keep your reader or your listener in mind.

We must work hard to help our reader understand the ideas and information we send.

Statistics: Words 225; s/p 1.6, w/s 8.0; passives 0%, Reading Ease 74.4, Grade Level 4.8

Limit your worries (V-11) *Technical Writing, An Introduction* *2009.12.01 © mns*

TECHNICAL WRITING—TOWARD A DEFINITION

This course is about Technical Writing. So, it's mainly a writing course.

I call it an "Introduction", because it's only a one-semester course. And this can be a big and detailed subject. I'll try to keep it clear, simple and useful to you.

But, what do people mean by "Technical Writing"? Can you think of a good, short definition? What does it mean to you today? Write 1 or 2 ideas here:

____

____

Well, it isn't easy to say, is it?

In fact, several Technical Writing textbooks do not offer any definition at all. Probably that's because <u>one definition cannot include all cases</u>. The dictionary has many definitions of the word "technical". Just look at them and you'll begin to see the problem.*

What makes writing "technical"? It can be technical <u>because it's about technical subjects.</u> In this course, we'll also learn to make our writing <u>technically correct.</u>

But we need a good, working definition. For our course, I offer one useful <u>definition</u>, one <u>description</u> of GOOD technical writing, and comments on eight (8) earlier attempts.

Memorize ONE good definition, and be prepared to write it down. Definitely, I will ask you for a written definition on the final exam.

I am interested in any new definition of Technical Writing that you can find or make, especially if it is better than the ones included here. Please let me know.

*You'll find some definitions of **"definition", "technical"** and **"writing"** on the following pages.

Readability Statistics: words 247; s/p 2.5, w/s 10.2; passives 0% FRE 62.3, GL 7.1

Toward a definition (V-23) *Technical Writing, An Introduction* *2009.11.11 © mns*

THREE KEY WORDS DEFINED*

(Toward a definition of technical writing)

definition *n.* **2.** the formal statement of the meaning or significance of a word, phrase, etc. *(4 def'ns given)* [RHWCD, 349b]

technical *adj.* **1.** pertaining to an art, science, or the like: *technical skill.* **2.** peculiar to or characteristic of a particular art, science, profession, trade, etc.: *technical details.* **3.** meaningful or of interest to persons of specialized knowledge. **4.** of, pertaining to, or showing technique. **5.** technically demanding or difficult: a technical violin sonata. **6.** concerned with the mechanical or industrial arts and the applied sciences: *a technical school. (10 def'ns).* [1434b]

writing *n.* **1.** the act of a person or thing that writes. **2.** matter written with a pen or the like: *His writing is illegible.* ...**7.** the style, form, quality, etc., of...composition. *(9 def'ns given)* [1511a]

* All definitions copied from *Random House Webster's College Dictionary* [RHWCD], Second Revised and Updated Random House Edition, April 2000.

Technical Writing

A Working Definition in Plain English

Technical writing is any writing that tells the reader how to do a job.

Good Technical Writing

A Description

Good technical writing helps the reader do a job well by providing enough of the right information in a form the reader can follow.

Mns

Statistics: Words 52, w/s 6.0; passives 0%, RE 100.0, GL 0.5

D.I.Y. Exercise:

Show your understanding.
Write the same ideas in your OWN language.

Add your own Student # _______________ and Name ______________________.

PART 2 - GOOD WRITING B.C.
–Before Computers!

The sentence

► Lesson 1 - Traffic Signs

Punctuation–A Famous Story

► Lesson 2 - How Long Should a Sentence Be?

Lesson 3 - Changing Passive Sentences to Active Form

► Passive Sentences for Re-Writing in Active (S-V-O) Form

Sentences: Review of Key Points & A Teachable Moment

► Faulty Return Address (Proofreading)

► Editing Exercise (Short Excerpt)

– Mechanical Engineering Research Report

Four Writing Skills We Need To Practise

Technically Correct Writing - A Quick Review of Core Grammar & Reference Information Section

Capital Letters - Chart

Punctuation - Summary

Active Grammar - Summary

The Twelve Tenses of English Verbs - Chart

Teaching Point:

Write technically correct English sentences.

Lesson 1: The Sentence
Traffic Signs

Very briefly, let's review some basics. At first, we learned letters, then words, then sentences. Every student reading this book has done all that. Fine. Here's an example:

I like ice cream.

Q. Is this is a good, correct English sentence? How do you know? Tell me now:

▷

▷

▷

Many students will answer that it has a **subject,** a **verb** and an **object.** They learned that this is the standard grammatical form of a complete, correct English sentence. In fact, **S-V-(and sometimes O)** is the standard structure of a correct English sentence.

In simple outline, we often write: **S - V - O**

Here, the Subject is "I". **The Verb is "like".** **The Object is "ice cream".**

Q. But how can we know, before reading, if some words are PROBABLY a sentence?
A. We just need to look for some **signs or signals.** I call them traffic signs or signals.

Q. What are these signals?
A1: The group of words begins with a Capital Letter (Initial Capital).
A2: It ends with a "full stop". 정지. The three "full stop" signs are:

Period (•) **Exclamation Point (!)** **Question Mark (?)**

So we can say, two signs or signals of a SENTENCE are:

1. Initial Capital (대문자) **2. Full Stop (점)**

Certainly, you have heard of the cities of Dae-gu (대구) and Dae-jeon (대전). Now, I invite you to visit **Dae-Jeom (대→점).** It's a City of the Mind, with great **traffic signs!**

Teaching Point: Always include these traffic signs in your sentences.

Punctuation

A Famous Story

woman without her man is nothing

An English professor wrote these words on the blackboard.

He told his students to punctuate the sentence correctly.

The men wrote: "Woman, without her man, is nothing."

The women wrote: "Woman: without her, man is nothing."

In this example, one might say,

"Punctuation is everything!"

Statistics: Words 55, para's 9, sent. 5; s/p 1.0, w/s 7.8; passives 0%, Reading Ease 68.7, Grade Level 5.6

Punctuation (Rev.) *Technical Writing, an Introduction* *traditional (mns)*

Lesson 2: The Sentence
How Long Should A Sentence Be?

In the first lecture, we learned that there are **traffic signs** that show us where a sentence begins and ends. They are: **1. Initial Capital (대문자)** and **2. Full Stop (점).**

Here is a new question: What's the shortest English sentence you can write?
Here are some typical answers:

Yes. No. Stop! Go! Run! Really? O.K.

Q: What traffic signs mark these seven (7) expressions as possible "sentences"?
A1: Each one begins with an Initial Capital Letter.
A2: Each one ends with a "full stop". 정지. Remember? The three "full stop" signs are:

Period (.) **Exclamation Point (!)** **Question Mark (?)**

Some experts would call each of these expressions a sentence. Others would say, only **Stop! Go! and Run!** are true sentences, because they have (*or,* are) main VERBS. (The *understood* subject, in each case, is YOU.) Probably everyone would agree that these expressions are short, common and useful. In writing, they LOOK like sentences.

We already know the standard structure of a correct English sentence.

S - V - O

Key Point: The VERB provides the ACTION, the motion, the main energy in any sentence. We could even say:

THE VERB IS THE MOTOR OF THE SENTENCE.

Let's say that out loud together: "The VERB is the MOTOR of the SENTENCE."

Exercise: Now, look at the following group of words. It's supposed to be a paragraph. Apply your knowledge: look for the verbs, and add traffic signals (initial capital letters and punctuation) to divide the words into correct, understandable English sentences.

After that, do the calculations required. We will look at the results together on the board.

How Long Should a Sentence Be?

How long should a sentence be perhaps this seems a strange question it isn't it's a major issue often neglected make your average sentence 10 words long isn't that very restrictive not really it means that if you write one sentence 15 words long then sooner or later you should write another sentence only five (5) words long average 10 words there's a lot of room for variety and flexibility.

The top line on this page is a title. How do you KNOW that, just by looking at it?

Title: 1. It's the top line. **2.** It's short. **3.** It's centered. **4.** It's in **bold**, black letters. **5.** All the main words begin with a capital letter (an initial capital). Notice: in this example, the writer uses the first words of the first line as the title. The title here is also a sentence—a question. So it ends with a question mark. The paragraph answers the question.

The "paragraph" under the title is all one long sentence. So, it's hard to read and understand. Your job is to make this writing easier to read and understand.

DO THESE STEPS IN CLASS!

(You may work with a partner.)

1. Insert punctuation and capitals to make sensible, correct shorter sentences.
2. Write your new sentences in a list on the next page. →
3. Count the number of words in each sentence. Write those numbers.
4. Add up the total number of words and count the number of sentences.
5. Write those two numbers in the blanks.
6. Calculate the average number of words per sentence.

Teaching Points:

Question: What are the teaching and learning purposes of this exercise?

Answers: **• to review sentence punctuation & Capitals &**

• to calculate average words / sentence.

How Long Should a Sentence Be?

Writing Exercise: Right here on this page, re-write the "paragraph" as individual sentences. **Count** the number of words and the number of sentences. **Calculate** the average number of words per sentence. Choice: you can include the title in your calculations, or not. How does that change the result?

1. How long should a sentence be?

2. Perhaps

3. It isn't.

4. It's a major

5. Make

6. Isn't that

7. Not really.

8. It means

9. There's

10. Title: Number of words? ____ Will you include them in your calculation, or not?

• ***Words ____, • Sentences ____ ►Average # of Words per Sentence (w/s) _____.***

Question: Are the sentences easier to read now? Circle YES / NO (I hope so!)

Write the date we did this exercise: ______________________

Sentence Punct., Caps., W/S Calc. Ex. *Technical Writing, An Introduction* *Exercise 2009.3 © mns*

Lesson 3: The Sentence
Changing Passive Sentences to Active Form

In the first lesson, we learned that there are **traffic signs** that show us where a sentence begins and ends. They are: **1. Initial Capital** and **2. Full Stop (대→점).**

In the second lesson, we learned that **the verb is the motor of the sentence;** and that **we should make our average sentence ten (10) words long.**

Here is a new question: What is the best kind of sentence for us to use in our writing?

We already know the standard structure of a correct English sentence:

S - V - O

Imagine this picture:

The boy kicked the ball.

Subject = boy **Verb = kicked** **Object = ball.**

This is a standard sentence. It is also an active sentence. Certainly, the boy is active—he's kicking the ball. But the SENTENCE is also in *ACTIVE form*. This means, it has an active verb and a ***forward-moving*** (left to right) order of ideas.

The action moves from the subject (S) through the verb (V) to the object (O).

(Technically, this verb form is called *active voice* (능동태). I mean, grammar teachers call it *active voice*. But don't worry too much about that special vocabulary. It's ***jargon***.)

Can we write the same information in a different sentence? Sure:

The ball was kicked by the boy.

Same picture. But this sentence is in PASSIVE form. The verb is in *passive voice* (수동태). The words are in a different order and there are two more words. Most surprisingly, the grammar and the real action in the sentence move in opposite directions!

The **grammar** goes Left to Right. The **ball is the subject** and **was kicked** is the **verb.** The **boy** is standing in his own little phrase ***(by the boy).*** (But he's NOT an object.)

However, the real-life action of the sentence moves Right to Left, from the actor, the boy (at the end of the sentence, on your right) back through the action, the verb, to the ball (at the beginning of the sentence, on your left). It seems there's a kind of friction or conflicting motion inside the sentence. Maybe that's one reason this passive sentence construction seems weaker than the active form.

But there's a bigger problem with passive sentences. People, such as scientists, engineers and office administrators use the passive form to **remove the people** from their sentences. Scientists, in an effort to sound "objective" say things like:

"The water was heated to 100 degrees Celsius." (Or, Centigrade)

Can you see a human, acting in this sentence? No. There is only the water, heating.

An office worker writes: **"Your letter was lost." Or, "Your letter got lost."**

Administrators love this kind of sentence. Can you see any people here? Who, exactly, lost the letter? Nobody. Maybe the letter became confused and "lost" itself. Getting lost is now the letter's fault. Nothing can be done about it.

Too often, people use passive sentences to avoid responsibility.

Instead, we could say, "I lost your letter." Or, "We lost your letter. Sorry. Can you send it again?" Then we could try to solve your problem &/or answer the letter. Better, isn't it?

To change a passive sentence to active form, just make sure that SOMEONE DOES SOMETHING. If there are no PEOPLE in the sentence, put them back in!

In this course, always try to WRITE SENTENCES IN ACTIVE FORM. Most writing teachers recommend this method. MS-Word's Spell-check will also remind you about it.

Here's an exercise, so you can practise changing passive sentences to active form.

Teaching Point: Write sentences in *ACTIVE* form.

Statistics: words 578; s/p 3.0, w/s 9.4; passives 3%, Reading Ease 79.7, Grade Level 4.4

Change Passive to Active *Technical Writing, An Introduction* *Lesson 3 of 3, 2009.3 © mns*

Passive Sentences for Re-Writing
In Active (S-V-O) Form

A passive sentence, correctly used, can tell us the action that produces the result.

Examples: The Mona Lisa was painted by Leonardo da Vinci.
The Statue of Liberty was donated to the United States by France.

A passive sentence, correctly used, can tell us the actor (who or what does the action).

Examples: The Mona Lisa was painted by Leonardo da Vinci.
The Statue of Liberty was donated to the United States by France.

A passive sentence can also tell us about materials (what something is made of).

Examples: The Eiffel Tower was constructed **of** iron beams.
The animated characters were made **of** clay.

Notice: The materials did not ACT to produce the result. Use of, not "by".

NOT: "The animated characters were made by clay."

(Actually, the clay dolls are made by people. But they're made of clay.)

That is: People made the dolls out of clay. [This is *ACTIVE* form: S-V-O.]

Exercise: Write these passive sentences in ACTIVE (S-V-O) FORM:

1) The Mona Lisa was painted by Leonardo da Vinci.

____

2) The Statue of Liberty was donated to the United States by France.

____

3) The Eiffel Tower was constructed of iron beams.

____

4) The animated characters were made of clay.

____

5) This exercise was completed very well by all the students.

____

Class # ______ Student #_______________ Name_________________ Date__.__.__

S-V-O Exercse (V-8) *Technical Writing, An Introduction* *2009.2 (2006)©mns*

Sentences: Review of Key Points

Begin with a **C**apital.

End with a period (•) _or_ other closing punctuation, (**!**) _or_ (**?**).

Main Verb—put one every sentence. (Can you put your _finger_ on it?)

Use *Active* Verbs. (Change passive verbs to active ones.)

Statistics: Words 40; s/p 1.4, w/s 5.8; passives 0%, Reading Ease 75.2, Grade Level 4.2

Sentences, Review Key Points *Technical Writing, An Introduction* *2008.9.26 © mns*

A Teachable Moment

At the end of my lesson on "Changing Passive Verbs to Active Form," a student handed me the following note:

My student card was left in a hostel.

I said, "OK. So send me a memo on the school's attendance system, and I'll mark you present.

"And by the way, _who_ left your student card in the hostel?"

The answer was a sheepish grin.

"Maybe you did," I continued. "So, I think your note should say:

I left my student card in a hostel."

In the active sentence form: ***Somebody does something.****

And takes responsibility for it, in conversation or in writing.

* See Richard Mitchell, ***Less Than Words Can Say***.

Statistics: Words 113, Sent. 10; s/p 1.2, w/s 8.3; passives 10%, Reading Ease 80.1, Grade Level 4.1

Teachable Moment (V-11) *Technical Writing, An Introduction* *2009.9 © mns*

FAULTY RETURN ADDRESS: A Real-Life Example

(Group Editing Exercise & Discussion)

The two lines below are part of the Return Address, or Sender's Address, printed in the top left corner of a business envelope. The envelope is used for sending out official mail from the department.

XXX 대학교 법정대학 원어민 연구실

English Porgram Office Collage of Law and Political Science XXX University

QUESTIONS

► **Can you see any problems or errors in English on line two? If so, what are they?**

-
-

► What impression do you get of the quality of that English program? **Is it a good impression?** Would you recommend this program to your friend? Maybe not! Suppose an English teacher who works there sees one of those envelopes. How to you think they will feel? Terrible. 기분안좋아요. What's the impression of that whole university? Not so good.

Well, it's easy to make mistakes. People are not perfect. Certainly, it's easy to make a typing mistake in English. The point is to find and fix mistakes before we send them out into the big world. How can we do that?

► **What key steps did the writer miss?**

ANSWERS

- Check the spelling of key words in a dictionary.
- Use the Spelling & Grammar checking tool in MS-Word.
- Show your writing to another person. Ask them to check it. (Proofreading)
- This is an English Program office. Probably some English teachers work there! It would be reasonable to ask an English teacher, maybe even a native English speaker, to check this item before printing 500 envelopes.

DISCUSSION

Now, there's a problem. We have a box of 500 envelopes with printing errors on them—or more than one box. What should we do? We could keep using the envelopes, including mistakes, until they're all gone. Or we can throw 500 or 1,000 new envelopes in the waste basket. If we do, we're throwing out money, too. What would you do? Will you fix the mistakes? Will you check your result before ordering new printing? **[Bonus Q: Why is the English printing so small?]**

Statistics: words 331; s/p 4.0, w/s 8.5; Readability: passives 2%, Reading Ease 77.6, Grade Level 4.5

Faulty Return Address (V-16) Technical Writing, An Introduction 2009.9, 07.8.20 © mns

MECHANICAL ENGINEERING RESEARCH REPORT

Excerpt for Editing

Here is the first sentence of some writing I received for professional English editing:

Since it is sometimes impossible to take samples for mechanical testing out of <u>the</u> structures in service, many research<u>es</u> attempted to evaluate the damage[s]* <u>of</u> structures non-destructively for in-situ monitoring [10-14].

Editing Instructions:

1. Count the number of words _____ and # of sentences ____ in these first three lines.
2. How long should a sentence be? Average: _____ words. Here, words/sent. = _____.
3. What do you <u>usually</u> do with a really long noodle? ______ _____! (Right. Me too.)
4. Can you do the same with this long "noodle" sentence? (Of course you can!)
5. Where's the best spot? How can you find it easily? *[HINTS: Punctuation, and, but....]*
6. Now make two good sentences out of this long, challenging one.
7. Write your two sentences below. (Which two words will you delete? And why?)

____

____

____

____

8. **"Researches"** is <u>ugly</u>! Put some <u>people</u> in, or use the collective singular, "<u>research</u>".
9. Consider the tense of the verb **"attempted".** What would be better?

______________________________.

10. A problem word pair here is **"damage*/damages".** Explain briefly the meanings of "damage" and "damages" so we can choose the correct word here. *[See your dictionary!]*

Damage = ____________________; Damages = ________________________

11. What's wrong with "damage <u>of</u>"? What should we change it to? _______________.
12. ***"In-situ"*** is Latin. Can you say it in <u>English</u>? So, why not say it in English?! Here are two ways: <u>on-</u>_____________ or <u>in -</u>______________. *[It's normal to use a hyphen for any compound adjective. However, RHWCD shows **in situ** as an American English word entry.]*

Statistics(V-13): Words 264, Sentences 32; s/p 3.2, w/s 7.4; passives 0%, reading ease 72.5, grade level 4.9

Engineering Excerpt for Editing *Technical Writing, An Introduction* *2009.11 (2002) Exercise © mns*

Four Writing Skills We Need To Practise

WRITING – "Writing" includes re-reading your written work with a critical eye.

PROOFREADING – Means marking things in the writing that need fixing.

EDITING – Means deciding HOW to fix the problems, large and small.

RE-WRITING – Means actually fixing those things that needed fixing.

For best results,
these activities
must be done again
(and again)
in a spiral,
or cycle.

Statistics: words 64; w/s 8.6; passives 0%, reading ease 62.3, grade level 6.6

Responding to Student Writing

[Proofreading & Editing]

"I tell my students that writing is largely a matter of fixing things. And that the better they get at fixing things the better they will get at writing. Now, fixing things requires reading. Students who do not learn to read their own papers with a discerning eye will not be able to fix things."

Source: (Katz, 1988, p. 111) in *Teaching ESL Writing*, Joy M. Reid, Chapter 8, page 205

Statistics: words 61; w/s 13.7; passives 0%, reading ease 82.1, grade level 5.2

4 Writing Skills *Technical Writing, An Introduction* *2008-08-28 © mns*

Technically Correct Writing
A Quick Review of Core Grammar
& Reference Information Section

HOW TO USE CAPITAL – 대문자 – LETTERS IN ENGLISH

USE A CAPITAL FOR	EXAMPLE	COMMENT
1. The first word of a sentence	We saw a movie last night. It was amazing!	**Capitalize** means use a big letter, not a small one.
2. Names of people	I met Cleopatra in my dream.	Wonderful!
3. Professional titles & Military ranks	I phoned Professor (Prof.) Kim. Commander Woo is a good man.	**Compare:** I saw a doctor. I saw Doctor Park.
4. Months, days & holidays	I was born in March. The package arrived on Monday. It snowed on Christmas Eve.	**Note:** Seasons are **not** capitalized: *spring, summer, fall / autumn, winter*
5. Place names: **city** **state / province** **country** **continent** **ocean** **lake** **river** **desert** **mountain** **school** **business** **street, etc.** **building** **park, zoo**	He lives in Montreal. She was born in Ohio. They are from Peru. Nepal is in Asia. They crossed the Pacific Ocean. Toronto is on Lake Ontario. The Amazon River is very long. The Sahara Desert is growing. Banff is in the Rocky Mountains. I go to Yeungnam University. I work for Samsung Electronics. He lives on Forest Hill Road. The exam is in Song Am Hall. We walked in Central Park.	**Compare:** She lives in a city. She lives in New York City. **Compare:** They crossed a river. They crossed the Rhine River. **Compare:** I attend university. I attend Stanford University. **Compare:** We went to a park. We were jogging in High Park.
6. Names of courses	I'm taking Accounting 101 this semester.	**Compare:** I'm reading about philosophy. I'm taking Philosophy 203.
7. Names of languages and nationalities	He speaks Spanish at home. It's a Korean custom to bow.	**Always capitalize** names of nationalities and languages.
8. Names of religions	Buddhism, Christianity, Hinduism, Islam and Judaism are major religions in today's world. Kamal is a Muslim.	**Always capitalize** names of religions.
9. The pronoun "I"	Yesterday, I fell off my bicycle.	**Always capitalize "I".**

Capitalization *Modelled after Azar, B.S. in English Grammar* *2010 © mns*

PUNCTUATION

The purpose of proper punctuation is to achieve clarity of meaning and expression. It helps the reader to get the right message from the words before him.

Punctuation need not conform to any set of rigid standards. Its purpose is to help you to express yourself on paper.

, THE COMMA

Use a comma between two adjectives: "What is desired is a pleasing, consistent appearance."

Use a comma to separate words or figures that might otherwise be misunderstood: "Instead of a hundred, thousands came."

Use a comma before and after *etc.*: "The store sells toys, hunting guns, etc., besides small electrical appliances."

Use a comma before and after *however*: "His wife, however, disagreed with him."

Do not use a comma before parentheses (brackets), but place the comma outside the closing parentheses.

. THE PERIOD

Omit periods after cent, per cent, nicknames and Roman numerals.

Omit periods from call letters of radio stations, organizations, political parties; CBLT, NATO, UNESCO, CCF, but use periods if a particular combination of letters happens to form a word without the periods: W.H.O. (World Health Organization); U.S. (United States).

Avoid double punctuation. The period does not combine with other major punctuation such as question or exclamation marks at the end of a sentence.

Place period outside closing parentheses if the parenthetical statement is only part of the sentence: "The train did not arrive until 9.45 (8.45 standard time)."

: THE COLON

Use a colon to introduce a direct quotation, a list of officers, or an enumeration of detail. It should be used with:

for example:
as follows:
to wit:
thus:

Do not combine the colon with the dash (:—), use either one, preferably the colon.

; THE SEMICOLON

The semicolon is to be used when a division in the thought requires more than a comma but less than a period:

"Editors should know good punctuation; what is more, they should watch for its faulty use in material submitted for publication."

The semicolon should also be used in a list, or the component parts of a complex sentence, as in the following:

"The election of officers resulted as follows: J. A. Smith, president; B. K. Ides, vice-president; L. P. Coster, secretary, and H. J. Donald, treasurer."

"The speakers were: L. M. Black, Modern Labels Ltd.; D. F. Brounson, Wholesaler Trading Corp.; F. B. Hyster, Canadian Frozen Foods Ltd."

— THE DASH

The dash is used to indicate a break, an abrupt stop, or to separate a parenthetical expression from the main thought:

"We wish our suppliers — particularly those who know we have a deadline to meet — would make deliveries on time."

"Pushing a button, handling a gauge, winding wire — whatever the process on which a workman is engaged — is only part of the job."

(THE PARENTHESES)

Use the parentheses to enclose a word or phrase distantly related to the subject matter:

"Pneumatic (forced air) systems have several advantages over other mechanical conveyors."

! THE EXCLAMATION MARK

The exclamation mark is used to indicate surprise, fear, irony or scorn. Use this mark sparingly, as too many exclamation marks will give the text the appearance of a dime novel. Avoid using two or more exclamation marks together.

? THE QUESTION MARK

Use the question mark if the subject matter is a direct or indirect question:

"How many firms were represented?"
"Was it the Pope who said: 'Our fears do make us traitors'?"

THE - HYPHEN

As a general rule, use the hyphen when the vowel is doubled. EXCEPTIONS: cooperation, cooperate, coordinate, coordination.

Hyphenate compound adjectives such as: machine-cut, rock-bound, die-formed.

Hyphenate: vice-president, attorney-general, secretary-treasurer.

Do not hyphenate: postwar, today, tomorrow, living room, dining room, nevertheless.

To form a plural of hyphened words add the letter *s* to the important element: fathers-in-law, hero-worshippers.

Hyphenate: half-circle, quarter-mile, half-title, by-laws, by-products, part-time.

Do not hyphenate compound of: bi, tri, semi, demi, as in: bimonthly, tricolor, semiannual, demijohn.

Do not use hyphen with the Latin prepositions ante, anti, inter, intra, post, sub and super as in: antedate, antidote, interurban, intramural, supernumerary.

Hyphenate first-class, second-class, when used adjectively.

Care must be taken not to confuse the qualifying word with the subject word: a Dutch cheesemaker, a Dutch wooden-shoe maker; old school-teacher, high-school teacher; small station personnel, small-station personnel.

THE APOSTROPHE ’

Use the apostrophe with such expressions as: four years' experience; eight hours' work.

Do not use apostrophe in plural form of letters or figures such as MPs, PCs, 1970s, etc.

The use of the apostrophe in possessive cases is recommended with the following exceptions:

1. Do not use when the following letter is an *s*
   James's scarf (wrong), too many sibilants.
   James' scarf (right), easier to say and read.
2. Do not use when the word is longer than two syllables:
   Demetrius's courage (wrong).
   Demetrius' courage (right).
3. Do not use in poetic or reverential contexts:
   Jesus's prayers were answered (wrong).
   Jesus' prayers were answered (right).

“ QUOTATION MARKS ”

It may be modern to depart, sometimes, from the just confines of grammar, or from the accepted rules of punctuation. But we should be careful not to muddy up the meaning of our written words.

Use double quotation marks before and after a direct quotation; use single quotation marks for a quotation within a quotation:

"I believe it was Dryden who said of Sir Francis Bacon:
'The world to Bacon does not only owe its present knowledge,
but its future too'."

If quoted matter is longer than one paragraph, use opening quotation marks at the beginning of each paragraph and closing quotation marks at end of the last paragraph. Example:

"The people who contacted me were very much concerned about the reaction of other residents.

"Despite their fears, I believe that we should proceed."

The positioning of punctuation marks in relation to closing quotes has long been a point of controversy. If the quoted matter forms the lesser part of a paragraph or sentence, a satisfactory solution is to place the punctuation mark outside the closing quotation marks:

She took her guests on a tour of her new house, acting on the premise that "everybody's interested in a home".

ACTIVE GRAMMAR

—A SUMMARY—

The Parts Of Speech and What They Do

Ask not: "What is it CALLED?"	Ask rather: "What does it DO?"
<u>**What it DOES**</u>	<u>**What it's CALLED**</u> (in "grammar speak")
NAMES a Person, Place or thing	NOUN *(thing)*
SHOWS action or existence	VERB *(Do♬Be, Do♫ Be, Do ♩...)*
ADDS information about a verb	AD•VERB
ADDS information about a noun	AD•JECTIVE
INTRODUCES a phrase	PREPOSITION
INTRODUCES a clause	CONJUNCTION *(joining)*
SHOUTS! Exclaims! Interjects!	INTERJECTION

ADDS still more information about a noun	ARTICLE *(a, the)*
VERB form *(-ing),* **working as a noun**	GERUND
VERB form *(-ing, -ed),* **working as an adjective**	PARTICIPLE
VERB **using two words** *(when one will often do)*	PHRASAL VERB *(get up)*
A small word, **showing relationship**	PARTICLE *(to; v + up)*

Three Main Verb Tenses*

"Tense means Time."

There are three (3) main TIMES – PAST, PRESENT and FUTURE. You must make clear which <u>**main**</u> time you mean. In grammar, **the verb shows time,** and technically speaking, we call it **tense.** "Tense" means "time". It's that simple.
We can refine ideas of time using still more tenses, but these 3 are essential.

It's worth your time to check your writing and get them right!

* English has 12 tenses in all: 3 main ones X 4 (simple, perfect, continuous & perfect continuous).

THE TWELVE TENSES OF ENGLISH VERBS

(A Quick Review of Core Grammar)

The first thing you need to know is that TENSE means TIME. Say it out loud:

"TENSE MEANS TIME."

There are three (3) main times that most of us use in daily life. If you can be really clear in talking and writing about these three main times, then I think fifty percent 50% of all your time communication problems will be solved.

THE THREE (3) MAIN TIMES ARE: PAST, PRESENT, AND FUTURE.

Here are some common time words that build up a picture of the three main times.

PAST	PRESENT	FUTURE
was	is	will be
before	now	later, after, soon
yesterday	today	tomorrow

ENGLISH HAS TWELVE (12) TENSES.

There are TWELVE, and only twelve verb tenses in English. But sometimes textbooks confuse us. Different textbooks call the same tense by a different name. Also, the names could tell us more clearly what each tense shows. I'll try to remove the mystery.

As you know, TWELVE can be written as three times four: 12 = 3 x 4. We have three main tenses. Their official, grammar names are: past, present and future. Under each main time, there are four variations. But those four variations are always the same!

That fact makes our job much easier. But it gets even easier than that! Actually, under each of the three MAIN TENSES, there are only three truly different variations. The fourth one just combines number two and number three on the list. Here's the chart:

PAST	PRESENT	FUTURE
simple	simple	simple
perfect, or *"finished"*	perfect, or *"finished"*	perfect, or *"finished"*
continuous, or progressive	continuous, or progressive	continuous, or progressive
perfect continuous *(combi)*	perfect continuous *(combi)*	perfect continuous *(combi)*

To read this chart for the PRESENT time, for example, we would say:

1. Simple present; 2. Present perfect; 3. Present continuous (*or,* present progressive) and 4. Present perfect continuous (*also known as,* present perfect progressive).

And there you have it, the whole "tense" story on one page. So, RELAX! You've got it!

Statistics: words 340, s/p 3.1, w/s 9.2; passives 7%, Reading Ease 81.8, Grade Level 3.9

Twelve Tenses *Technical Writing, An Introduction* *2009.9 © mns*

PART 3 - GOOD WRITING A.D.
–After Digital

What Your Computer Can Do For You

Create a Shortcut on the Desktop

Acceptable Fonts For This Course

Add these Names to your Spell Check Dictionary

Readability Scores, C.A.R. Statistics, The "After-math" Of Writing

What are C.A.R. Statistics?

► Display / Enable Readability Statistics In MS-Word 2007 & 2003

► Understanding Readabilty Statistics: Daewoo Shipbuilding Co. (DSME)

The "After-math" of Writing: Classic Technical Writing Tools
& How to Display them on your Page

► C.A.R.S. Summary & Three (3) Review Questions

► Two Famous Finger Exercises For Typing In English

Summary of Writing Course So Far

Teaching Points:

Use The Technology To Improve Your Work.

C.A.R. Statistics are the "after-math" of writing.

WHAT YOUR COMPUTER CAN DO FOR YOU

Your computer can 'magically' improve your English mark, a lot. Just ask it to help you! It can help you to be a much better writer. It can help you to get a good grade.

USE YOUR GRAMMAR & SPELL-CHECK TOOL

Your English-language Word Processing program HAS a Spelling and Grammar-checking tool. **Turn it on.**

USE your **grammar & spellchecker** often. PAY ATTENTION to what it tells / asks you.
Note: For better or worse, each decision is still up to you!

Microsoft Word is the standard word-processing program for this course.

Use MS-Word Online Help (?) to get instructions on setting up your personal computer.

WHAT YOUR GRAMMAR & SPELL-CHECK TOOL CAN CHECK FOR YOU

1. Sentence Capitals	(use them)
2. Name Capitals	(use them)
3. Correctness of verb forms	(e.g. final **s** on 3rd person singular, present tense)
	(e.g. past tense verb forms, regular & irregular)
4. Correct tense sequence	(what comes before what; what follows what)
5. Matching Subjects & Verbs	(this includes adding **s** to plural nouns)
Matching Objects & Verbs	(this includes matching number, gender and case)
6. Spellings	(often, more than one spelling is possible)
7. Idioms	(these are fixed forms; don't re-invent them)
8. Spacing	(use standard English spacing)
9. Passives	(replace them with active forms)
10. Punctuation	(provides order; adds to meaning)

You can add a **full grade** to **every piece** of your writing by **using your spell-checker** to **find** your errors. You must then **act to correct them,** of course.

Use your spell-check **again** just before you print any assignment. You'll be surprised!

Statistics: Counts: words 251, Averages: s/p 1.6, w/s 9.2; passives 0%, reading ease 77.5, grade level 4.7

Computer AID (V-12) *Technical Writing, An Introduction* *09.11 (20/4/ 03) © mns*

Create a desktop shortcut
for an Office program or file

Applies to: Microsoft Office Access 2007, Excel 2007, InfoPath 2007, OneNote 2007, Outlook 2007, PowerPoint 2007, Project 2007, Publisher 2007, SharePoint Designer 2007, Visio 2007, Word 2007

Create a desktop shortcut for an Office program

When the Microsoft Office programs are installed, you have the choice to create a desktop shortcut for the individual Office programs. However, if you don't create a desktop shortcut at the time that you install Office then decide that you want a desktop shortcut later, you can easily create one.

1. Click **Start**, point to **All Programs**, point to **Microsoft Office**, and then point to the Microsoft Office program for which you want to create a desktop shortcut.
2. Right-click the name of the program, point to **Send To**, and then click **Desktop (Create shortcut)**.

A shortcut for the program appears on your desktop.

Create a desktop shortcut for an Office document or file

You can also create desktop shortcuts for specific Office files or documents.

1. Click **Start**, then point to **Documents**.
2. Browse to the document or file for which you want to create a desktop shortcut.
3. Right-click the name of the document, point to **Send To**, then click **Desktop (Create shortcut)**.

A shortcut for that document or file appears on your desktop.

http://office.microsoft.com/en-us/help/HA100777101033.aspx

Acceptable Fonts For This Course

<u>FONT</u> means the <u>Style</u> and the <u>Size</u> of the letters or characters.

The <u>minimum</u> acceptable sizes of computer fonts for this course are:

Serif fonts: Times New Roman, 12
Garamond, 12 *or* Century, 11

Sans serif fonts: Arial, 12 *or* Arial, 11
Helvetica, 12 *or* Helvetica, 11
Microsoft Sans Serif, 11 *or* Microsoft Sans Serif, 10
Verdana, 11 *or* Verdana 10

These FONT size prescriptions apply to the **main text**, or "body" of any assignment.
I do accept that footnotes and contact information on a letterhead may be smaller, but readable.

Your Name on a **Letterhead** should be bigger and **bolder.**

You CAN request individual approval for other fonts. They should be equal to or better than the fonts I have specified, in **reading ease, clarity and size**.

I DO <u>NOT</u> ACCEPT <u>ANY</u> BATANG in English. *It just isn't a good font* for me to read. The Roman letters are too thin. Their lateral spacing is uneven. The VERTICAL (up/down) spacing between lines is BIG!

However, BATANG in 한글 Hangul is terrific! 좋아요! It's a really good font for fitting words on the page. **<u>Experiment</u>** to find your favorite font. Below is a test for Batang. Batang Che *is even **WORSE.*** (<u>Terrible</u>!)

CAPITALS, *Italics* and Bold. CAPITALS, *Italics and* Bold.	Size 11
CAPITALS, *Italics* and Bold. CAPITALS, *Italics and* Bold.	Size 12
CAPITALS, *Italics* and Bold.	Size 14

CAPITALS, *Italics and* Bold.

Statistics: words 230; s/p 2.7, w/s 7.7; Readability: passives 0%, Reading Ease 69.1, Grade Level 5.5

Acceptable Fonts (V-6) *Technical Writing, An Introduction* *2009.11 © mns*

ADD THESE NAMES TO YOUR SPELL-CHECK DICTIONARY IN MS-WORD

Here's how:

1) Download this page and save it as an MS-Word document.
2) On the Toolbar, click Tools, Spelling & Grammar.
3) For most words in this list, the spellchecker will show you a box saying "Not in Dictionary", and show you the word in RED.
4) At the Right side of the box, find & click "Add to Dictionary." It's the third button.
5) After you finish the list, your Spellchecker will always check these words for you. It will ACCEPT your correct spellings, or ask you to fix any mistake.
6) Correcting a typing or spelling mistake is easy. When spell check shows you ONLY ONE, correct version, just click "change". When it gives you options, choose the BEST version from the list and then click "change". Let the computer replace the word for you! Isn't technology wonderful?

Busan
Daegu
Geoje Island
Gyeongbuk
Gyeongsan
Jeju
Mechanical Engineering
Mother
Seoul
Yeungnam University
Your hometown
Your future employer

Statistics: Words 160; s/p 2.0, w/s 9.7; passives 0%, Reading ease 81.9, Grade level 4.2

Spellcheck Names *Technical Writing, An Introduction* *2009.4.7 © mns*

READABILITY SCORES

C.A.R. STATISTICS

The "After-math" Of Writing

Concepts and Page Design
2009.8.26 © MNS
Graphics Courtesy of Clip Art

C.A.R. Statistics (V-8) *Technical Writing, An Introduction* *2009.8 © mns*

What are C.A.R. Statistics?

Amazing but true—**"CAR" statistics** are NOT about regular CARS, or even Baja cars!

What are <u>these</u> cars? They're mathematical **C.A.R.S.,** parked inside your computer!

In fact, **they are <u>Readability scores</u> you can turn on in Microsoft Word—**

Imagine! Using <u>Math</u> to help you write well in <u>English</u>!

In this Technical Writing course, we'll use the initial letters ***<u>C.A.R.</u>*** to stand for:

> **<u>Counts</u>** - Words, Characters, Paragraphs and Sentences
>
> **<u>Averages</u>** - Sentences per Paragraph (s/p); Words per Sentence (w/s) and Characters per Word (c/w)
>
> **<u>Readability</u>** - Passive Sentences (as a %); Flesch Reading Ease (as a percentile) and Flesch-Kincaid Grade Level (number of years in school).

We could say **"<u>C.A.R.S.</u>"**, to mean <u>**R**eadability **S**cores</u> or <u>**R**eadability **S**tatistics</u>.

Use my CAR! Remember these three (3) main kinds of statistics. Microsoft Word's "Readability scores" program can automatically count, calculate and communicate very useful information about your piece of writing. Use the Spelling and Grammar Checking Tool and the ***C.A.R.*** statistics will appear automatically. But you have to turn them on!

HOW?

Instructions follow on how to activate (turn on) this very useful sub-program.

First, let's look at the ***"full <u>C.A.R.</u> statistics"*** <u>for this page</u>, up to this colon<u>:</u>

<u>COUNTS</u>:

Words 199, Characters 1078, Paragraphs 15, Sentences 15

<u>AVERAGES</u>:

Sentences per Paragraph (s/p) 1.6, Words per Sentence (w/s) 8.4, Characters per Word (c/w) 5.2

<u>READABILITY</u>:

Passives 0%, Flesch Reading Ease (FRE) 53.9, Flesch-Kincaid Grade Level (FKGL) 7.8

Now, do you see what I'm driving at?

Good! Then let's put the show on the road!

Readability Stats (V-30) Technical Writing, An Introduction 2009.11.13 © mns

Display / Enable Readability Statistics, Or Readability Scores

Applies to: Microsoft Office Word 2007* ("Enable Readability Statistics")

1. Click the **Microsoft Office Button** , then click **Word Options 옵션 (I)** button.
2. Click **Proofing: 언어교정.**
3. Make sure **Check grammar with spelling** is selected.
4. Under **When correcting grammar in Word**, select the **Show readability statistics** check box √: 문장난이도표시**. Then click 확인.**

To Use Spell Check, Grammar Check & Statistics Tools in Word 2007

1. Click 검토 Tab.
2. Click 맞춤법 및 문법검사.
3. The C.A.R. Statistics box will appear automatically when Spell check is complete.

Applies to: Microsoft Office Word 2003 ("Display Readability Statistics")

1. On the **Tools** menu, click **Options**, and then click the **Spelling & Grammar** tab.
2. Select the **Check grammar with spelling** check box.
3. Select the **Show readability statistics** check box, and then click **OK**.
4. On the **Standard** toolbar (toolbar: A bar with buttons and options that you use to carry out commands. To display a toolbar, press ALT and then SHIFT + F10.), Click **Spelling and Grammar** .

When Microsoft Word finishes checking spelling and grammar, it displays the Readability scores / statistics. These show information about the reading level of the document.

http://office.microsoft.com/en-ca/word/HP101485061033.aspx#1

* My thanks to **Stephanie White** for researching how to turn on these statistics in English, in **MS-Word 2007**.
* Thanks again to Prof. Mo Chung for his help in matching the English and Korean instructions.

Readability statistics (V-B2) *Technical Writing, An Introduction* *2009.11.10*

Understanding Readability Statistics

Daewoo Shipbuilding & Marine Engineering Co., Ltd.

Seoul, South Korea

// DSME Company Description

Daewoo Shipbuilding & Marine Engineering (DSME) has secured a berth as one of the world's top shipbuilders. DSME <u>builds</u> special-purpose ships, <u>repairs</u> ships, and <u>constructs</u> plants. A contractor to major oil companies, DSME constructs various vessels, offshore platforms, drilling rigs, floating oil production units, submarines, and destroyers. It specializes in liquefied natural gas *[LNG]* carriers and oil rigs. Established in 1978 as the shipbuilding and marine engineering division of Daewoo Heavy Industry, DSME sailed off from its former parent in 2000. It became publicly listed on the Korean Stock Exchange a year later. Korea Development Bank (KDB) is DSME's largest stockholder and holds 31% of the company. **//**

Statistics (// Profile //): Words 109; s/p 7.0, w/s 15.1; passives 14%, Reading Ease 39.8, Grade Level 11.4

http://www.hoovers.com/dsme/--ID__147900--/free-co-profile.xhtml

Review of Readability Statistics & Questions on Content

1. What is the average number of words per sentence in this brief, company description or profile? ***(Hint:** What do the statistics tell you?)*

2. Among Korean high school graduates, how many will be able to read and understand this information? ***(Hint:** How many grades to finish high school?)*

   ______________________________ will be able to do so.

3. Name three (3) of DSME'S business activities. *(Hint: find three <u>action</u> verbs.)*

   DSME ______________________________

4. General knowledge: Who owns or controls Korea Development Bank?

   ______________________________ own(s) or control(s) KDB.

5. According to the statistics below, how easy or difficult are these five questions to read and understand? (**Note:** this doesn't mean you know the answers…!)

   ____

Question Statistics: Words 111; s/p 1.5, w/s 9.3; passives 0%, Reading Ease 70.8, Grade Level 5.7

DSME Profile & Stats (V-8) Technical Writing, An Introduction Exercise 23/2/09 © mns

The "After-Math" of Writing
Classic Technical Writing Tools &
How to Display Readability Statistics on your Page

We could say, "C.A.R. statistics are the "after-math" of writing!

What does that mean?

We can USE this math immediately after writing, to improve our work.

Classic Technical Writing Tools

Readability statistics are now classic "technical" writing tools. "
Microsoft calls them "Proofing Tools"— tools for proofreading and making repairs.

But why "classic"?
- Dr. Rudolf Flesch invented them over 60 years ago by.
- They've become standard writing / editing tools in MS-Word.

Maybe I should call them *"Classic C.A.R. Statistics"!*

How to Display Readability Statistics on your Page

Adding C.A.R. statistics to a page is NOT "normal" writing procedure.

It's our secret weapon for improving our writing. *Shh...*비밀. (Only your classmates will know. And your seniors. And me. And millions of other good writers around the world.)

But let's make it a little easier to use these statistics. I don't like driving full cars. They're too heavy, and driving performance is reduced. Let's travel lighter.

From now on, let's choose only some of these statistics.

- ▶ For this writing course, show them at the bottom of your page.
- ▶ HINT: First, copy them by hand on a scrap of paper.
- ▶ Type them on one line, in a smaller font, *in italics* and centered.

Follow the model below:

Statistics: words 218; s/p 1.6, w/s 8.0; passives 4%, Reading Ease 73.5; Grade Level 5.0

After-math & Display *Technical Writing, An Introduction* *(Rev. 15) © 2009.11 mns*

AFTER-MATH

COUNTS

AVERAGES

READABILITY

STATISTICS

This page is a summary of the Readability Scores, or Statistics—a classic technical writing tool available to you in Microsoft Word.

The short-form (acronym) **C.A.R.S.** tells you the main headings.

Of course, to benefit, you must turn on and use these writing tools.

REVIEW QUESTIONS

Q. What are C.A.R. Statistics?

Q. What makes them "classic" writing tools?

Q. Why can we call them the "after-math" of writing?

Statistics: Words 73; w/s 9.1; passives 0%, Reading ease 82.1, Grade level 4.0

After-math, Recap *Technical Writing, An Introduction* *2009.8 © mns*

Two Famous Finger Exercises For Typing In English

Now is the time for all good men to come to the aid of their party.
Now is the time for all good men to come to the aid of their party.

[Words/sentence 16.0; RE 100.0, GL 3.1]

The quick brown fox jumps over the lazy dog.
The quick brown fox jumps over the lazy dog.

[Words/sentence 9.0; RE 94.3, GL 2.3]

There's something special bout the second example.
Can you see what it is? Look at the sentence for 30 seconds.

Try typing **each sentence five times** on your PC.
Your English keyboarding skills will probably improve quickly.

"Practice makes perfect." Or better, certainly.

Statistics: Words 115; s/p 1.2, w/s 8.4; passives 0%, Reading ease 86.3, Grade level 3.3

Summary of Writing Course So Far

SENTENCES and How to Make One:

1. A SENTENCE <u>must</u> have a Verb, and a Subject.
2. A SENTENCE <u>must</u> begin with a Capital and end with some full stop (. ? !)
3. A SENTENCE in our writing <u>should average 10 words</u> in length.
4. ACTIVE sentences are MORE POWERFUL than passive sentences.
5. USE ACTIVE VERBS in your sentences. (Few exceptions are needed.)
6. GOOD SENTENCES are error-free, *ACTIVE* in form, and not too long.

YOU CAN MAKE GOOD SENTENCES OR GOOD EXCUSES. RARELY BOTH.

(And both are not needed.)

PUNCTUATION:

7. PUNCTUATION MARKS make sentences complete and understandable.
8. USE punctuation marks as TRAFFIC SIGNALS—what should "eye" do?
9. Please visit the **New City of the Mind, 대→점•**

PARAGRAPHS:

10. **SHORT** paragraphs are easier to read than <u>v e r y   l o n g</u> paragraphs.
11. Our EYES really LIKE the WHITE SPACE between paragraphs.
12. SEPARATE paragraphs clearly, using one of three standard methods.

TECHNICAL (COMPUTER) TOOLS:

13. TOOLS in Microsoft Word can help us:
    a. **Counts** can easily count our <u>words</u>, <u>sentences</u> and <u>paragraphs</u>.
    b. **Spelling and Grammar Checkers** can help <u>find</u> and <u>correct</u> errors.
    c. **Statistics** can help us make our writing easier to read and understand.
14. You must SELECT and ACTIVATE these classic, "technical" writing TOOLS.
15. Your can configure these sub-programs to suit your working style.
16. These correction tools have FAULTS. They are NOT always reliable.
17. We must improve OUR OWN SKILLS to make the best editing decisions.
18. These tools cannot replace a HUMAN proofreader or editor. Find one!

► *This page is written mostly in Batang 10. What do you like or dislike?*

Statistics (V-8): words 250; s/p 1.2, w/s 8.3; Readability: passives 11%, Reading Ease 73.3, Grade Level 5.1

Summary so far *Technical Writing, An Introduction* *24/08/09 © mns*

PART 4 - COMPLETING A RESUMÉ FORM

Job Applications: Resumes, Letters & E-mails - An Introduction

Resumé - Two (2) Definitions & Three (3) spellings
An English Resumé Form from a Korean Company
Advantages and Disadvantages of Fixed, Set Resumé Forms
Differences Between Korean & North American Resumé Styles
Differences Between Real & Practice Job Applications
Readying Your Resumé, "for Real"

Job Applications: Résumés, Letters & E-mails – Introduction

It is essential to prepare a good résumé and job application letter. You need them. But students have little or no experience with writing resumes, letters or e-mails.

Question: How many e-mails do you write in one month? Fewer than five? Over 10? Today's students send (and receive) text messages on mobile phones. Times change. However, most companies ask people to apply for jobs via e-mail, or on paper, or both.

Consider these questions and answers:

►What result should your letter, your resume or your e-mail achieve?
A1. Each of them should communicate key information clearly, briefly and accurately.

►What effects should they avoid?
A2. They should avoid confusing or annoying the reader.

►In each case, how should I begin?
A3. Begin with a clear purpose. State your purpose in line # one.

►What should I include?
A4. Include essential facts. Advertise personal qualities.

► What should I omit?
A5. Omit all errors and excuses.

►How should I organize the material?
A6. How would you like to receive this information?

►How long should my letter or my resume be?
A7. Use one side of one page for each.

►How do I finish?
A8. Politely and professionally. And *sign* your letter by *hand.*

►How can I judge if my letter is suitable?
A9. Read it out loud. Does it represent you positively and accurately?

►Why can't I just copy a letter from the Internet? Can't any native English speaker, or any English professor, just write my letter for me?

A10. A native speaker's letter can easily be a bad letter. (They didn't take this course!) And no other person can present you as well as you can present yourself.

There is another problem: if the letter you send is too far above your own level, then, sooner or later, the reader will be disappointed. And you may both feel uncomfortable. So it is probably wise to write a letter that shows your own best abilities.

Trust yourself.

Statistics(V-16): Words 330, sent. 50; s/p 1.9, w/s 6.3; passives 0%, Reading Ease 73.8, Grade Level 4.5

Job Applications Intro *Technical Writing, An Introduction* *2009.9.21 © mns*

Resumé – Two (2) Definitions & Three (3) Spellings

The long and the short of it...

Resume, a dictionary definition

résumé ***or*** **resume** ***or*** **resumé** *n.* **1.** SUMMARY **2.** a brief written account of personal, educational, and professional qualifications and experience, as that prepared by a job applicant. [1795-1805; <F., n. use of ptp. of *résumer* to RESUME]

Random House Webster's College Dictionary, page 1126b
Second Revised and Updated Random House Edition, April 2000.

Resumé, a shorter definition

A résumé is a brief written account of personal, educational, and professional qualifications and experience.

[Learn this short definition.]

Statistics: Words 95; s/p 1.7, w/s 9.0; Readability: passives 0%, FRE 29.8, Grade Level 11.3

Resume

Resume	No	※

Photo (3 x 4)	Name			Department Applied	Preferred Region
	Last Name		Priority1		
	First Name		Priority2		
	ID Number		Phone		
	Address		Cell Phone		
			E-Mail		

Education						
Period	Name of School	Major	Graduate (Yes/No)	Degree	Location	G.P.A
. . ~ . .						/
. . ~ . .						/
. . ~ . .						/
. . ~ . .						/
. . ~ . .						/

Military Service					
Period	Military Name	Branch	Rank	Recipient of National Merit Award	Reason for no service
. . ~ . .					

Career				
Company Name	Duties	Position	Period	Reason for Resignation

Family Status					
Relation	Name	Age	Occupation	Position	Live Together

Foreign Language						Licenses/Certification		
Test Name	Score	Conversation Level				Date	Place of Issue	License/Certification
TOEIC			Top	Middle	Bottom			
TOEFL			Top	Middle	Bottom			
JPT			Top	Middle	Bottom			

Foreign Countries: Experience		
Country	Period	Contents
	. . ~ . .	
	. . ~ . .	

ETC	
Computer Programs You Can Use	Serve the Community

With thanks to TaeguTec for the original form

Date: 200 . .

ADVANTAGES & DISADVANTAGES of FIXED, SET RESUME FORMS

ADVANTAGES

For the Company, Institution or Government Agency

1. They can ask for all the information they want.
   (They don't forget to ask anything.)
2. It's easy to compare applications.
   (The same information appears in the same place.)

For the Applicant

1. He/she knows what information the employer wants and does not want.
2. Applicant doesn't need to create a resume.

DISADVANTAGES

For the Company, Institution or Government Agency

1. Form may omit some useful category of info.
2. Required information may be illegal to ask for in some countries.
3. Company may not update the form to fit new hiring needs.

For the Applicant

1. Spaces may not be big enough to write in required info.
2. Some items may not apply to some applicants.
3. No space may be available to add some relevant info.

* * *

Statistics: Words 135; w/s 8.8; Readability: passives 0%, FRE 70.1, Grade Level 5.6

Resume Forms (V-6F)   Technical Writing, An Introduction   08.02.23 © mns

Differences between Korean and North American Resume Styles

There are a few important differences between standard Korean and standard North American resumes. These include the KIND of information required and the ORDER of presentation. Find out and follow the method required by each company you apply to.

Photo

In Korea, schools and businesses normally **require** a 'face' photo on their applications.

In North America, it is **often illegal** for employers to ask for a photo. The main reason is to prevent discrimination against any applicant based on age, gender (sex), race or hairstyle. The law says these features are not directly related to qualifications or ability to do the job.

In fact, some North Americans who say they want to work in Korea feel very uncomfortable about sending a photo on their applications. If they don't send one, they won't get the job. A few feel so strongly, they even decide not to apply. Problem solved.

Time Order

In Korea, the usual method is to follow time order in the Education and Career or Work Experience sections. For example, in Korea we present middle school, high school, and university education in that order. It's called **chronological order**.

In North America, the usual method is the opposite. Employers want to know your **highest** grade in school, or your **most recent** work experience FIRST. Then we work back in time. This is called **reverse chronological order**.

Family Ties

In Korea, it is normal to list members of one's immediate family, giving their names, ages, jobs or professions and even whether they live together or not.

In North America, we think, "you are hiring me, not my family. So, all of that information is none of your business!"

Perhaps neither approach is all right or all wrong. Each method is just the custom of the place. To get the job, it's wise to follow the local custom, wherever possible.

Statistics (V-6): Words 316, Sentences 24; s/p 2.6, w/s 12.6; passives 12%, reading ease 58.8, grade level 8.1

Resume Differences K vs NA *Technical Writing, An Introduction* *2009.09 © mns*

DIFFERENCES BETWEEN REAL JOB APPLICATIONS AND PRACTICE VERSIONS PREPARED FOR CLASS

There are some important differences between **real** job applications and the **practice** versions of Resumés and Cover Letters that we prepare for class.

REAL JOB APPLICATIONS

Photo

Send only good quality photos, taken by a professional studio. Get a haircut first. Wear proper business clothes: for men, a shirt, necktie and suit jacket; for women, something tailored and modest.

Resumé

Use your Citizen I.D. number, 주민번호, on your real resumé and other official documents.

Cover letter

You need NOT add Readability statistics to a real job letter.

(What would be the purpose?)

Order of Presentation

Staple your "Cover Letter" ON TOP. Your Job Application Letter introduces you and your Resumé. Its position says,

"Read me first!"

PRACTICE VERSIONS IN CLASS

Photo

No photo is required. Some students add a fun, informal photo so the teacher will recognize their face. The photo should be in focus, and recent – not your freshman photo, please.

Resumé

Use your Student I.D. number on your practice resumé. The instructor needs this number to record your grade.

Cover letter

Add Readability statistics to your letter, on one line at the bottom of the page. These statistics show that a) you used Spell Check and b) you turned on the Statistics, as required. They may also show that c) you looked at the statistics and d) perhaps used them to help you improve your letter.

Order of Presentation

The instructor may decide to collect and grade your Cover Letter and Resumé individually, as separate items, or together as a core Job Application package.

Statistics: words 253, sentences 18; s/p 2.2, w/s 12.1, passives 0%, Reading ease 65.9, Grade level 6.9

Readying Your Résumé, "for Real"*

Review of Key Points

- COMPLETE THE FORM.
- ANSWER EVERY QUESTION.
- CHECK SPELLING & CAPITALS.
- KEEP IT NEAT.
- ADD A BUSINESS-STYLE PHOTO.
- PUT YOUR JOB APPLICATION LETTER ON TOP.

Statistics: Words 32; w/s 3.8, passives 0%, FRE 59.4, FKGL 5.9

31 October 2008

RESUMES—A COMMENT

When I talk to you about resumés, this isn't all about grades.
It isn't really, or mainly, about English, either.

This is about DOING stuff effectively in the big world—succeeding in your chosen field: engineering, teaching, trade, law, environment, or fashion design.

Just get it done, and done well.

You may notice that there are three (3) different spellings of **resumé** on this page: no accents, one accent or two accents, one on each **e**. Any of these spellings is acceptable. PICK ONE, and use it.

* **Note:** "For Real" is a very informal, conversational expression. It is rarely written. But people say it when they are serious about something. And applying for a real job is a serious business. Let's be "really ready," then relax and enjoy the process.

Statistics (Comment & Note): Words 133; s/p 2.0, w/s 10.8, passives 8%, FRE 67.6, FKGL 6.5

Readying your resume(V-6) *Technical Writing, An Introduction* *2009.11, 08.11 © mns*

PART 5 – BASIC JOB APPLICATION OR "COVER" LETTER

"I am Writing...." A Universal Letter Starter

Four (4) Musts - A.S.A.P. - An Aid to Memory

Basic Job Application Letter - A.S.A.P. Model

Action Verbs for Letters & Resumes

How to Produce the Three (3) Standard Paragraph Styles

10 Cover Letter Mistakes to Avoid

◎ 커버레터 작성시 피해야 할 10 가지 실수

Memo (Mini) to Students

Subject: Reading your Job Application Letters & Resumes

Favorite Filler Phrases To Delete

Tell Me Now !

Spell-check Testing: Comments On A Student's Job Application Letter

Checklist – Presentation Requirements for your Basic Job App Letter

"I Am Writing..."

A Universal Letter Starter

Starting a letter or e-mail is difficult for most people.
"Goodness! What should I say?"

I recommend you begin with something actual, factual and absolutely true. And use an *ACTION VERB*. It gets you—and your letter—***m o v I n g!***

"I am writing..." is a WONDERFUL beginning. Use it to start any letter or any writing project.

For Example: I AM WRITING...

to apply for the _________ position you have advertised.
to complain about the poor quality of your product.
to congratulate you on your new job/promotion.
to inform you about our elegant new perfume.
to offer new, low-cost insurance on your credit card debt.
to suggest a new dessert to add to your menu.
to thank you for the wonderful (gift / dinner....)

Of course, you could start even more simply, and in some cases, with more emotion.

For Example: **Congratulations on your new job!**

You've just delivered your main message, in five (5) words!

Statistics (V-7): words 165; w/s 8.0, passives 0%, FRE 75.1, GL 4.7

FOUR (4) MUSTS

Cover Letter **An Aid to Memory** **Job App. Letter**

A.S.A.P.*

1. The main purpose of a "cover letter" is to get / gain / secure an **interview.**

☎ ☏

2. Here are **the four (4) things you "must" do** in your Job Application Letter:

- **A**pply for the position.
- **S**tate your qualifications. ☆
- **A**sk (politely) for an interview.
- **P**rovide contact information. ☎

☆ **Qualifications include:**

a) academic achievement

b) work experience

c) personal qualities and values

d) language skills &/or work/travel abroad.

☎ **Provide complete, correct contact information** (*or,* briefly, **CCCI**).

☏ ☎ ☏

► It's time to write your own job application letter. To make a good, basic letter, follow the model on the next page. Save your letter as an MS-Word document.

* **A.S.A.P.** usually means *As Soon As Possible.* (It's an ***acronym***, or short form made of the initial (first) letters of key words. Here, A.S.A.P. is also a ***mnemonic device***, an aid to memory.

Statistics (V-21): Words 120; s/p 2.0 w/s 10.5; passives 0%, FRE 74.3, Grade Level 5.5

JAL – Four (4) Musts *Technical Writing, An Introduction* *2009.3.30 © mns*

BASIC JOB APPLICATION LETTER – A.S.A.P. MODEL

Name & Address of
Receiving Person
Name of Company
 # Street Address
Include Postal Code *[You do want it to get there **on time**, don't you?]*

*[**Date:** Write the month in FULL, as a word: e.g. 27 October 2012]*

Dear Sir / Advertiser / Design Manager / Mr. Park *[Choose ONE.] + Punctuation*: or ,

A I am applying for the Entry Level Mechanical Engineering position you have advertised.

S I will graduate from Yeungnam University in June 2015, with a major in automotive frame design using CAD-CAM. In May 2012, I won the *"Top Design"* prize, sports car division, in the Apprentice Automotive Design Competition (AADC) held in Daegu.

I would like to contribute to designing the new generation of hybrid-fuel sports cars that HSDK motors is planning to produce.

A I would be happy to show you my design portfolio at an interview.
References are available on request. My resume is attached.
I look forward to / hearing from you / your reply. *[Choose ONE.]*

Thank you. *[Optional]*

Sincerely, / Yours truly, *[Choose ONE.]*

[NOTE: On paper, you will sign in this space.]

P *Your Mailing Address*
with Postal Code
Your Phone Number
Your E-mail Address

[NOTE: There are three reasonable places to put all your personal contact information: at the TOP, in the MIDDLE, (letter body) or below the Signature, in an INFO BLOCK.

Please follow the structure or method on this page first. You will soon see the purpose for it.]

►New! ADD Statistics, on ONE LINE – but only for this Assignment, not for your REAL job application letters. "C.A.R." Statistics are your secret weapon here! [See PART 4.]

(V-14) Statistics: Words 265; s/p 1.8, w/s 9.4; passives 4%, Reading ease 66.6, Grade level 6.3

Action Verbs for Letters & Resumés

For Three Skill Sets Only

Research Skills

- Analyzed
- Clarified
- Collected
- Compared
- Conducted
- Critiqued
- Detected
- Determined
- Diagnosed
- Evaluated
- Examined
- Experimented
- Explored
- Extracted
- Formulated
- Gathered
- Inspected
- Interviewed
- Invented
- Investigated
- Located
- Measured
- Organized
- Researched
- Reviewed
- Searched
- Solved
- Summarized
- Surveyed
- Systematized
- Tested

Teaching Skills

- Adapted
- Advised
- Clarified
- Coached
- Communicated
- Conducted
- Coordinated
- Critiqued
- Developed
- Enabled
- Encouraged
- Evaluated
- Explained
- Facilitated
- Focused
- Guided
- Individualized
- Informed
- Instilled
- Instructed
- Motivated
- Persuaded
- Simulated
- Stimulated
- Taught
- Tested
- Trained
- Transmitted
- Tutored

Technical Skills

- Adapted
- Applied
- Assembled
- Built
- Calculated
- Computed
- Conserved
- Constructed
- Converted
- Debugged
- Designed
- Determined
- Developed
- Engineered
- Fabricated
- Fortified
- Installed
- Maintained
- Operated
- Overhauled
- Printed
- Programmed
- Rectified
- Regulated
- Remodeled
- Repaired
- Replaced
- Restored
- Solved
- Specialized
- Standardized
- Studied
- Upgraded
- Utilized

http://www.quintcareers.com/action_skills.html#technical

Accessed Feb. 09

How to Produce the Three (3) Standard Paragraph Styles

Use the proper method to produce the three (3) standard styles of paragraph divisions:

The first and oldest is INDENTATION, or INDENTED STYLE. This means you insert a gap or space before the first words of the paragraph.

The proper way to INDENT your first line is to use the TAB key. The TAB key is located on the left side of the keyboard. Press this key ONCE to move the cursor in "jumps" of about 7 spaces. On your computer keyboard, the TAB KEY has 2 arrows on it, showing that you can "tab over" to either the left or the right.

Do NOT, repeat NOT, use one, or two, or many little strokes on the spacebar to indent paragraphs. It's a bad method. The correct method is to use one stroke of the TAB key. You can set the tab stop position to please yourself.

The **TAB-INDENT method** was standard on the manual typewriter. It is still the method used in many books. Through hundreds of pages, it saves space and paper.

These paragraphs on indented style follow the tab-indent method.

* * *

The second method is called BLOCK STYLE. This means we insert one or more BLANK LINES between paragraphs. The first line of each paragraph begins at the left margin. There is NO indentation.

To insert a blank line at the end of each paragraph, press the ENTER KEY twice. Many people like the white space between paragraphs. It's restful to the eye.

This is a newer method. It became popular with the increased speed of the electric typewriter. It's very efficient.

These paragraphs on block style follow the block-style method.

* * *

The third standard paragraph method combines the first two. This can be called SEMI-BLOCK or MODIFIED BLOCK STYLE. In this method, the writer indents the first line AND separates paragraphs with a blank line (white space).

Some people like this combination style. The plus, or upside is, it does make paragraph separations clear. The minus, or downside is, it takes the most time and energy. In fact, it demands as much of both as the first and second methods combined.

These paragraphs on modified block style follow the combined method.

WARNING TO THE READER! The layout of this page is very unusual. The purpose is to show three (3) paragraph styles on the same page. **It's an exception!** DO NOT do this in your writing. For each letter or report, choose **ONE** style only and use that one.

Statistics: Words 420; s/p 3.0, w/s 10.1; passives 5%, FRE 78.4, GL 4.8

Letters, Para's (V-21) *Technical Writing, An Introduction* *2008 © mns*

10 cover letter mistakes to avoid

When it comes to job applications, cover letters are often the last thing jobseekers think about. But with fierce competition for the best jobs, there's no excuse for writing any old letter just so you can paperclip your resume to it.

In fact, many employers are now treating cover letters as mini job applications in their own right, and savvy jobseekers are following suit, creating carefully crafted letters that announce their suitability for the job - and compel employers to hire them.*

"Thanks to the high standard and volume of job applications received by employers, I think there's definitely been a shift in the importance of cover letters," says Emma Buxton, director of Buxton Pratt Consulting. "The cover letter no longer takes a back seat to the resume; employers see the cover letter as an important indicator of whether or not you've read the job advertisement, and are genuinely interested in the job you've applied for."

Indeed, according to Buxton, jobseekers have around 30 seconds to impress potential employers with their cover letter - or not. "Cover letter mistakes are costly because they reduce the likelihood that your resume will be read and spoil your chances of gaining a job interview," she says.

So, if you're serious about making a first impression that lasts, avoid these common cover letter no-nos:

1. Skipping a cover letter entirely
To prevent unnecessary disappointment, always include a cover letter with your job application, unless the application instructions specifically request you don't.

2. Opening with an offensive salutation
In order to use the most appropriate salutation, you need to discover exactly who to address your cover letter to - and that means doing your homework. Once you've determined the contact person's name, you'll be able to work out whether to address them as Mr, Mrs, or Ms. If in doubt, always use a gender-neutral salutation.

3. Ignoring grammar and spelling mistakes
Sometimes it's hard to know what changes to make to a cover letter when you've been working hard on it. Before you send your cover letter to a potential employer use the spell-check feature available with most word processing software; then ask a friend to have a look at it with fresh eyes and to suggest improvements.

4. Leaving out the job title or job reference
When a potential employer reads your cover letter, they want to know what job you've applied for. Failing to quote the job title or job reference in your cover letter suggests an inability to follow instructions, and can often result in your application not being processed.

5. Addressing the wrong person or company
Even first-class cover letters can end up in the rejection pile if they never reach the right recipient. So, before you post or email your job application, always set a little extra time aside to check the contact details on your cover letter against those provided in the job ad.

6. Being too casual or familiar
To make sure that your cover letter hits the right note, you need to use the right style, tone and language. So when it comes to crafting your masterpiece, always be formal, professional, and concise. But don't think 'formal' has to mean 'stiff': while using text message shorthand is likely to result in outright rejection, adding a little personality can make your cover letter read better.

7. Attaching an informal photo
While you might have fallen in love with that hot party snap and have convinced yourself that your cover letter won't be as effective without it, if it would be right at home among the clubbing pages of your favourite street press, then think carefully before you attach it to your cover letter - especially if an accompanying photo wasn't requested.

8. Spamming multiple employers
No potential employer wants to see a string of competitors' email addresses at the top of your cover letter - it makes your job application feel lazy and directionless even if it's not. Hiding potential employers' email addresses by listing them in the Bcc field can also backfire. Instead, personalise each message and email one employer at a time.

9. Using an unprofessional email address
If your personal email address is sexxxylicious_81@yahoo.com or similar, consider setting up an email account with a more professional name for the purpose of job-hunting. Also, displaying your full name to email recipients is preferable to displaying only your first name or nickname, and make sure your custom email signature is professional - these are all the little extras that potential employers notice.

10. Not revising an old cover letter
If you haven't updated your cover letter in the past year or when your responsibilities or qualifications changed, it's very important that you update it before you apply for your next job. This is one of the biggest blunders that potential employers will be on the lookout for; an out-of-date cover letter suggests indifference or lack of attention to detail, and will ultimately lose you a chance at the job

Published: 07 November 2007

Source: http://content.mycareer.com.au/advice-research/resume/cover-letter-mistakes-to-avoid.aspx

* *Underline emphasis added, mns*

커버레터 작성시 피해야 할 10가지 실수

취업지원자들은 취업지원서를 작성할 때, 커버레터를 중요하지 않은 것으로 생각하는데, 그것은 큰 오산이다. 좋은 일자리를 위한 치열한 경쟁 시, 커버레터를 당신의 이력서를 채우는 단순한 레터로만 생각하고 있다면 그것은 잘못된 생각이다.

사실 많은 고용주들은 커버레터를 "작은 취업지원서"로 간주하고 있으며, 지원자들도 그 직책에 대한 자신의 적합성을 잘 드러나게 하기 위해 커버레터를 정교하게 만드는 추세이다.

"훌륭한 자격을 갖춘 많은 취업지원자들 덕분에, 커버레터가 상당히 중요하게 변해 왔다." 라고 Buxton Pratt Consulting 원장인 Emma Buxton 은 말한다. "커버레터는 더 이상 이력서 뒤쪽의 한 자리만 차지하는 것이 아니라 지원자가 채용공고를 숙지했는지, 그리고 지원한 자리에 대한 흥미가 있는지에 대해 고용주가 판단하는 중요한 지표가 된다."

Buxton 에 의하면, 실제로 지원자가 커버레터로 잠재적 고용주에게 강한 인상을 남길 수 있는 시간은 고작 30 초에 불가하다. 아니, 그 보다 더 짧을 수도 있다. "커버레터를 작성할 때, 실수를 범하면 매우 큰 희생을 동반한다. 왜냐하면 그 실수는 고용주로 하여금 당신의 이력서를 읽고 싶은 마음을 감소시키고, 결국, 인터뷰 기회를 놓치게 하기 때문이다."라고 그녀는 말한다.

그래서 좋은 첫인상을 오래 동안 남기고 싶다면, 아래의 커버레터 작성시 해서는 안 될 것들을 반드시 피하도록 하라.

1. **완전히 커버레터 빼기**
   지원서 요강에 커버레터를 빼라는 지시가 없으면 취업지원서에 반드시 포함시켜라.

2. **무례한 인사말로 시작하기**
   적절한 인사말을 사용하기 위해, 누구에게 커버레터가 읽혀질 지에 대해 정확히 파악하고 있어야 한다. 다시 말하자면, 커버레터를 읽을 대상자를 정확하게 미리 알고 있어야 한다는 말이다. 그 사람의 이름을 안다면, Mr, Mrs, 또는 Ms 라고 해야 할 지도 알 수 있을 것이다. 만약 의심스럽다면, 성별이 구분되지 않는 인사말로 시작하는 것이 상책이다.

3. **문법과 맞춤법 무시하기**
   커버레터 작성에 너무 심취해서, 때때로 고쳐야 할 점이 잘 보이지 않을 때가 있다. 그래서 커버레터를 잠재적 고용주에게 보내기 전에는 워드 프로세서에 있는 맞춤법 확인 기능을 사용하고, 친구로부터 새로운 시선으로 검토를 받고, 보완할 부분이 없는지 조언을 구하여야 한다.

4. **직책이나 추천서 누락하기**

잠재적 고용주는 커버레터를 읽을 때, 어떤 직책에 지원했는지를 알고 싶어한다. 커버레터에 직책이나 추천서 언급을 누락하는 것은 지시사항을 따라 할 능력이 없다는 것을 드러내는 것이고, 그 지원서는 바로 쓰레기통으로 가게 된다.

5. **회사이름이나 수신자 잘못 적기**

만약 적절한 수신자에게 전달이 되지 않는다면, 아주 잘 작성된 커버레터도 탈락자 파일로 들어가는 경우도 있다. 그러므로 지원서를 우편이나 이메일로 보내기 전에 항상 충분한 시간을 갖고 커버레터에 있는 수신자나 연락처 정보가 모집공고와 다르지 않은지 자세히 살펴 볼 필요가 있다.

6. **너무 격식 없이 친근한 척 하기**

커버레터가 가장 효과적인 역할을 하게 하기 위해서는 바른 형식, 어조 그리고 바른 단어를 사용하는 것이 바람직하다. 최고의 작품을 만든다는 점에서, 커버레터에 써야 하는 문체는 항상 공식적이고, 전문적이고, 간결해야 한다. 그러나 공식적이란 말을 딱딱하다는 말로 생각하지는 마라. 문자 메시지 보낼 때 줄여 쓰는 표현을 커버레터에 쓴다면, 결과는 명백한 탈락으로 나타날 것이다. 그 반면에 약간의 개성이 나타나는 표현들은 관계자가 커버레터 읽는데 도움이 될 것이다.

7. **비공식적인 사진 붙이기**

어느 신났던 파티장에서 찍은 스냅사진이 마음에 들어서 만약에 그 사진이 없으면 커버레터가 효과적이지 못할 것 같다는 생각이 강하게 들더라도, 커버레터에 그 사진을 붙이는 것은 다시 생각해야 한다. 특히 사진을 첨부하라는 요구가 없을 경우에는 커버레터에 비공식적인 사진을 붙이기 전에 다시 생각해야 한다.

8. **한꺼번에 여러 회사에 보내기**

어떤 고용주들은 커버레터 위의 일련의 경쟁자들의 이메일 주소를 보고 싶어 하지 않는다. 이것은 당신이 게으르고 뚜렷한 목적이 없다는 것을 보여준다, 행여 그것이 사실이 아니라고 해도, 그리고 숨은 참조로 잠재적 고용주들의 주소를 감추는 것도 예기치 못한 결과를 불러올 수 있다. 그러므로 각 메시지마다 차별화하고, 한 번에 한군데씩 보내는 것이 바람직하다.

9. **프로답지 못한 이메일 주소 사용하기**

만약 당신의 이메일 주소가 sexxxylicious81@yahoo.com 이나 이것과 비슷한 것이라면, 지원한 직책과 좀 더 관련된 프로페셔널한 이름의 이메일 계정을 하나 새로 만드는 것을 고려하라. 그리고 수신자에게 당신의 성과 이름이 모두 나타나게 하는 것이 성이나 닉네임만 보여지는 것 보다 더 효과적이다. 그리고 이메일의

자동 서명도 프로페셔널한 것인지 확인하기 바란다. 이와 같은 사소한 것들도 잠재적 고용주에게는 판단의 자료가 된다.

10. 오래된 커버레터 수정하지 않기

새로운 직업에 지원하기 전에 반드시 커버레터를 수정하라. 만약 작년에 쓴 커버레터를 새롭게 수정하지 않았거나, 승진이나 기타의 이유로 책임범위나 능력이 변경되었을 때는 반드시 오래된 커버레터를 수정해야 만 한다. 수정되지 않은 커버레터는 잠재적 고용주가 눈 여겨 찾고 있는 지원자의 실수 중 하나이다. 수정되지 않은 커버레터는 세세한 것에 대한 주의부족이나 무관심을 나타낸다. 결국은 채용의 기회를 잃게 할 것이다.

출판: 2007 년 11 월 7 일

Source: http://content.mycareer.com.au/advice-research/resume/cover-letter-mistakes-to-avoid.aspx

MEMO re JAL 17 October 2008

TO: All Technical Writing Students

FROM: Michael Shapiro, Course Professor

Date: 17 October 2008

Subject: Reading your Job Application Letters & Resumes

FIRST, I am pleased that most of you have learned how to produce a well-organized letter page.

SECOND, many of you follow the ASAP and/or AIDA guidelines I gave you.

THIRD, most of you do sign your letters by hand, in ink.

FOURTH, many of you provide readability statistics, as I required. Some of these are genuine. Some are not.

> **I consider statistics INVALID when the letter contains spelling errors.**
>
> REASONING: Spell Check should FIND those errors. And you have the opportunity to CORRECT them. That is, IF you USE the Spell Check program. The Readability Statistics are available ONLY AFTER you run the Spell Check Program. So, if there are errors, your statistics are invalid, and probably BOGUS. Bogus means fraudulent. It means they are a lie. I give grades only for real performance.

FIFTH, Job Application Letters and Resumes are useful to you ONLY if the receiver ACTUALLY READS THEM. If your **font is too small**, nobody will read them. Certainly, I will not. Sometimes I can grade based on FORM. But then I cannot help you with CONTENT. Do you think your letter is an eye-testing chart? Then, maybe change your major to Optometry.

Did you have to increase the size of this memo to read it? Or use a magnifying glass? NUISANCE, isn't it?
Perhaps I should save pages next semester and print everything in font size 8. What do you think? Good idea?

Meanwhile, Happy Pepero Day!

Statistics (V-3): Words 270; s/p 2.6, w/s 8.3; passives 0%, Reading Ease (if you can see it!), 74.0, Grade level 5.0

Mini Memo re JAL *Technical Writing, An Introduction* *2008.11.11 © mns*

FAVORITE FILLER PHRASES

TO DELETE FROM JOB APPLICATION LETTERS

My name is Hong Gil Dong. *So what?!* Why are you writing? Why am I reading this?

I was born I Daegu in 1983. Oh, groan. Boring. Snoring. Is this a biography?

I have many experiences. FOR EXAMPLE? State your WORK and related experience.

I am better than the other candidates. WELL, the READER will decide that. Not you. Give some FACTS TO SHOW HOW, and in WHAT, you are superior, or more suitable. Besides, nobody likes a person who brags too much, or says they are so much better.

"I am having learned about English conversation course." REALLY? Lucky you. This course, by contrast, is about WRITING **correct** English, not talking nonsense.

"I would like to come to an interview at your convenience." HOW considerate!

> LISTEN! You can BET that the interview, if it happens at all, will be at the interviewer's convenience. If it is NOT convenient for them (and sometimes it isn't) that is still THEIR scheduling problem.
>
> The truth is, it must be convenient, OR AT LEAST POSSIBLE, for **both** parties. Otherwise, the interview CANNOT take place.
>
> Just don't waste time with FILLER words! Letter FILLER is ALWAYS inconvenient. It wastes my time and yours! Spare me.

Statistics (V-3): Words 210; s/p 2,6, w/s 5.2; passives 0%, Reading ease 76.6, Grade level 3.8

Filler Phrases, JAL *Technical Writing, An Introduction* *2009.2 © mns*

TELL ME NOW!

LINE ONE of your writing, any writing, is your first, best hope to talk to your reader. In a Job Application Letter, apply for that job in line one.

Most people miss this golden opportunity. So, YOU can be first in line!

You can say: **1) "I am writing to apply for the position of …." OR**
2) "I am applying for the position of …."

Instead of actually APPLYING, most people try to be "polite", or they try not to seem greedy, or they try to show they're eager.

So, they write: "I am interested in the position. (That's nice. And so what?)

"I would like to apply." (And WILL you? WHEN?)

You could write: "When I saw your ad, I was so excited, I could hardly breathe." (Please breathe.)

I suggest you begin your letter with a FACT, not an emotion. And not all facts are created equal.

For instance: "STX is a wonderful company." (True. But please wait— Write that sentence when they PAY YOU to advertise for them.)

Your Application Letter is YOUR letter. ADVERTISE YOURSELF!

You can do worse: "My father always buys Hyundai cars." (Is your father applying for this job? It's an entry level position.)

Or even, "Although I've never applied for a job before…." (Shoot me NOW!)

To begin your letter, there are ONLY TWO ACCEPTABLE OPTIONS in this course.

You can say: 1) "I am writing (to you) (to apply)…." OR,
2) "I am applying …." Then name the position.

After the course, you can write anything you like.

Meanwhile, whatever is on your mind, TELL ME NOW.

Statistics (Rev. 7): Words 267; s/p 1.6, w/s 7.6; passives 2%, Reading ease 83.5, Grade level 3.5

J.A.L. Tell Me Now! *Technical Writing, An Introduction* *2009.2 © mns*

Spell-check Testing: Comments

On A Student's Job App. Letter, 30 Oct. 2008

Exact quote, from a Job Application Letter, paragraphs three (3) and four (4):

I feel queit comfortable woking with students. Therefore,I'm pleased to find this job opprtunity and write this letter.

Thank you for spending time to review my resume.I will waiting for your respondse.

Same sentences, Spell-Checked, Grammar-Checked, Fixed, with real statistics:

I feel quite comfortable working with students. Therefore, I'm pleased to find this job opportunity and write this letter.

Thank you for spending time to review my resume. I will wait for your response.

Statistics: Words 34; w/s 8.5; Readability: passives 0%; FRE 71.3, GL 5.4

Notice that the Spelling and Grammar Check Tool has caught and often suggested repairs for four (4) spelling errors, plus two (2) spacing errors, plus one grammar error. I think that a letter applying for a language teaching position should be error-free.

Notice also that the true statistics for this section are much better than those you claim for your whole letter, which were:

"States: words 199; w/s 15.1; Readability: passives 0%, Reading Ease 45.1; Grade Level 10.4"

In this course, I REQUIRE you to activate and use these helpful writing tools.

I also recommend honest, accurate work. It can be refreshing. And easier to sign.

Sincerely,
Michael Neil Shapiro
Your Technical Writing Professor

Checklist – Presentation Requirements
for your
Basic Job Application Assignment

- **Make** your Job Application Letter ONE page long. Exceptions should be RARE.
- **Place** Job Application Letter on Top of Resume. It's a "Cover" Letter, remember?
- **Staple** all of your Job Application pages together. Use one staple in Top Left corner.
- **Sign** your letter by hand, in black or blue ink. It's a personal and a legal document.
- **Show** KEY Readability Statistics on ONE line at the bottom of the letter.

This **training step** will tell me:

a) that you've turned them on – this is a basic course requirement!
b) that you've probably USED Spell Check, and
c) that you may be considering how to improve your letter.

If I find spelling or grammar errors, I'll consider you have NOT used spell-check.

This also implies that your Readability or C.A.R. Statistics are BOGUS (false).

You can easily gain extra points on this assignment by using these very useful technical tools available to you in MS-Word. You've already paid for them!

NOTE: DO NOT INCLUDE READABILITY STATISTICS in letters you actually send out to employers or graduate schools. Keep and USE these statistics as your own "secret weapon" for better writing skill.

"Readability" here means "level of difficulty". How hard is it for the reader to read and understand your letter?

Statistics (V-11) : Words 218; s/p 1.5, w/s 10.2; passives 0%, FRE 64.9, GL 6.7

Checklist, Basic Job App. *Technical Writing, An Introduction* *2008.10.14 © mns*

PART 6 - E-MAIL JOB APPLICATIONS

Send An Effective E-mail

E-mail Etiquette Lesson: Subject Line is Essential.

More E-mail Etiquette: Greet, Sign off, Signature block

Do Not Send Messages All in Capitals - It looks like SHOUTING

Send An Effective E-Mail Job Application - Checklist & more

An E-mail Request, First Prepared on MS-Word & Spellchecked!

How To Send A Successful E-Mail Message

Teaching Point:

Send a correct and effective e-mail.

E-mail Etiquette Lesson
"Subject Line is Essential"

ETIQUETTE means good manners.

Some people call good **Internet** manners, **"Netiquette".**

Showing good manners in e-mail means:

- informing your reader
- addressing them by name
- keeping your messages short, polite and clear.
- signing off politely

When you COMPOSE an e-mail, you see 2 boxes: To and Subject.
When you RECEIVE an e-mail, you see 2 words: Sender and Subject.

It is essential to fill in the subject line.

WHY?

Your reader wants to know:
- •Is this for me? (To)
- •What is it about? (Subject)

He or she must decide:
- •How urgent is it?
- •Should I open it at all?

People base these decisions on the sender and subject information.

People protect their computers by DELETING messages from unknown senders.
People protect their work time by DELETING messages with no Subject line.

So, If you want someone to OPEN your message, give them a good reason.

And give them a good reason to READ your message. Catch their attention!

State your Subject. Tell your Topic.

Your Subject line is your NEWS HEADLINE

Catch Your Reader's Attention!

Statistics: Words 181, sentences 20; s/p 1.2, w/s 7.4; Readability: passives 0%, FRE 76.0, GL 4.5

E-mail (V-12) *Technical Writing, An Introduction* *2009.9.24, 2007 © mns*

More E-mail Etiquette

You can find lots of good advice on netiquette by doing an Internet search.

Right now, we are focussed on using good e-mail etiquette when we apply for a job. It's not much different, really, from showing good manners in person, or to a friend.

GREET YOUR READER

In e-mails, business or personal, it's polite and proper to begin with a greeting. In Job Applications, use formal style: Dear Mr. Jones, followed by a comma**,** or colon**:** For people you know, you can use: Dear Peter, Good Morning, Hae Jin, or Hi, Mark! Your level of formality depends on how well you know the person.

SIGN OFF

In business e-mails, you **must** "sign" (type) your name at the end, even if it's only "John". Most people appreciate this courtesy in personal messages, too. We <u>know</u> your name is at the top as Sender. But good manners remain in fashion.

CREATE A SIGNATURE BLOCK

Many e-mail programs allow you to create a standard <u>signature block</u> that gives your Company Name, Job Title, mailing address and phone number(s): ***CCCI.***

You can even make a "signature" that looks like handwriting! Your e-mail program can automatically add this "block" of information to the end of every message. Or it gives you the option to add these two items, or not. It's polite. It's efficient. Learn how to do these useful things. Check your e-mail's "Options" or "Help" menus.

Statistics (V-3): Words 237; w/s 10.8; Readability: passives 5%, RE 71.4, GL 5.9

Do Not Send Messages All In Capitals

USING ALL CAPITALS IN E-MAILS

LOOKS LIKE SHOUTING!

IT'S A BAD METHOD.

DON'T DO IT.

Statistics: words 22, sentences 3; s/p 1.0, w/s 3.3; passives 0 %, reading ease 100.0, grade level 0.0

대문자만 써서 메시지를 보내지 마세요.

E-mail 을 보낼 때 대문자로만 문장을 쓰는 것은

고함을 지르는 것처럼 나쁜 행동이니 절대로 하지 마세요.

With thanks to Eun-hee Choi, "Euphrasia" and Prof. Lee, Won-Kyoung for their translations.

E-mail Etiquette *Technical Writing, An Introduction* *2009.9 © mns*

Send An Effective E-Mail Job Application

Check these items!

√ **Add a Subject Line**

√ **Copy your Cover Letter Content**

√ **Add your phone number**

√ **Attach your Resumé**

√ **Check the receiver's e-mail address**

√ **Send.**

More Detail

1. ADD a **subject line**. Write:

APPLICATION + Competition # + Job / Dep't & Your Name

2. Just COPY and PASTE your saved **basic letter content** into your e-mail.

   Notice: Your **Letterhead** format will NOT work in e-mail —yours or his. It will usually be a mess. **Do not use it!**

3. ADD your **phone number** at the end of your message.

   You want them to call, so give them your number!

4. ATTACH your **resumé**. (Opening it is the reader's option.)

5. CHECK the receiver's e-mail address again, carefully.

   It is very easy to make a small mistake. (Application will fail.)

6. SEND your e-mail application.

7. CLEAR your **inbox** so you can receive incoming e-mail.

8. CHECK your **inbox** for any failed delivery. Or a *REPLY!*

Statistics: Words 127; s/p 1.5, w/s 6.0; passives 0%, Reading Ease 75.8, Grade Level 4.1

AN E-MAIL REQUEST

NOTE: **The writer first prepared this e-mail on MS-Word & Spellchecked it!**

To: proffice@skshipping.com
From: writewell@ynu.ac.kr
Subject: SK Calendar Request
Date: 19 Jan 09

Dear PR Officer:

I am writing to request one (or possibly two?) of your calligraphy calendars for 2009.

My wife and I find Korean calligraphy beautiful.
It would be so nice to have examples on our wall during the whole year.
The second copy would be a wonderful gift for us to give.

Thank you for considering this request.

My address is:

Michael Shapiro, Associate Professor
School of Mechanical Engineering
Yeungnam University
214-1 Dae-dong, Gyeongsan-si
Gyeongsangbuk-do 712-749, R.O.K.

Michael Shapiro

P.S. *SK Shipping Company kindly mailed two calendars. We were glad to have them.*

Statistics (V-3): Words 120; s/p 1.1, w/s 9.3; passives 0%, Reading Ease 61.3, Grade Level 7.0

How to Send a Successful E-mail Message

(EXPLAINED IN ACTIVE LANGUAGE)

WRITE IT & SEND IT

▷ **Give it a "headline", or <u>subject</u> line.**

▷ **State the purpose.**

▷ **Provide accurate information.**

▷ **Organize information logically—help the reader understand it.**

▷ **Use language that is as simple as possible, but as complex as necessary.**

▷ **Say exactly what you mean.**

▷ **Tell the reader what <u>action</u> you want him/her to take, and when.**

▷ **Know when to stop.**

▷ **Send the message on time.**

▷ **Always save a copy in "sent messages".**

FOLLOW-UP

Check that the person received your message. Ask: "Did you get my e-mail?"

Check in person, by phone, or by sms/text message. (Do <u>not</u> check by e-mail...!)

Statistics: Words 112, sentences 14; w/s 6.8; Readability: passives 0%, FRE 76.5, GL 4.2

E-mail (V-12) *Technical Writing, An Introduction* *2009.8, 07.6 © mns*

PART 7 - IMPROVE YOUR JOB APPLICATION LETTER

Teaching Point:

Design Your Own Job Application Package

★ Graded Assignment – CLR & Resume 20% ★

☎ Model Job Application Letters
from
Technical Writing Course Graduates ☎

&

"Why writing a job application letter
is not a useful task for me now"

Improve Your Job Application Letter

A Key Assignment

You have written a basic Job Application (Cover) Letter. Now let's improve your Letter. (*Upgrade Leganza!*) Here's how:

• **Add a Competition Number & Job Name as a Headline.**

Companies often ASSIGN a competition number to each job they advertise. They use that number to send your application to the right department and person. You must use it, too. Add the Competition Number & Job Name, centered and bold, like this:

Competition # 87213 – Design Engineer

We just did this in our e-mail job applications, in the subject line. Do you remember? Here, insert the "headline" after the "To" address, and before, "Dear Mr. Kim,"....

• **For this class assignment, we will create a special competition number.**

This number will identify YOU, so your teacher can record your 'A' grade. (You hope!) First, write your **class number**, then **dash,** then your **student number.** Put the Job Title on the next line, also bold and centered. **NOTE:** Use the "center" symbol on the toolbar. It's quick and easy. DO NOT use the TAB key for centering. It is not exact.

Example: A student in Class 1180 writes:

Competition # 1180 – 12345678
Design Engineer

• **More Improvements**

• **Leave space** for your Signature after "Sincerely," or "Yours truly." [ENTER x 5]

• **Type your name** so anybody can read it. Some signatures aren't readable.

• **Position your Contact Information (CCCI) – at the top!** It's a possible location.
In fact, we will soon make a CCCI Letterhead, for a more professional appearance.

• **Be sure to use your Spellchecker and Readability Statistics tools.**

• **See Part 4** for detailed instructions on how to turn on these useful tools.

• **Spell check your page** after each improvement.

• **Update** your **"C.A.R."** statistics.

• **Save** your **resume, basic & revised** job application **letters** (JAL) on your computer.

• **Create** a new FOLDER for these Job Application Core Documents.

• **Use** your **basic job application letter** for e-mail applications – just "copy and paste."

• **Use** your **letterhead version JAL**, which we'll make next, for applications on paper.

Statistics (V-10): Words 330; s/p 2.2, w /sentence 8.7; passives 0%, Reading Ease 67.8, Grade Level 5.9

Improve Your J.A.L. *Technical Writing, An Introduction* *2009.9 © mns*

Job Application Letter – Advanced Model –Content & Statistics

Your Name
Your Mailing Address
With Postal Code
Your Phone Number
Your E-mail Address

Name & Address of
Receiving Person &/or
Name of Company
 # Street Address
Include Postal Code *[You DO want it to get there **on time**, don't you?]*

[Date: Write the month as a word: October 27, 2012]

► ***New!*** ***Competition # 0212 - 12345678***
Job Title Applied For

Dear Sir / Advertiser / Design Manager / Mr. Park *[Choose ONE.] + Punctuation*: **or** ,

I am applying for the Entry Level Mechanical Engineering position you have advertised.

I will graduate from Yeungnam University in Feb. 2013, with a major in automotive frame design using CAD-CAM. In May 2008, I won the *"Top Design"* prize, sports car division, in the Apprentice Automotive Design Competition (AADC) held in Daegu.

I would like to contribute to designing the new generation of hybrid-fuel sports cars that HSDK motors is planning to produce.

►***Note! OMIT any mention of resumé here. List it ONLY as an ENCLOSURE.***

I would be happy to show you my design portfolio at an interview. References are available on request.

I look forward to / hearing from you / your reply. *[Choose ONE.]* Thank you. *[Optional]*

Sincerely, / Yours truly, *[Choose ONE.]*

► *John Q. Kim* ***New!*** *[SIGN by hand, with a BLACK PEN.]*

► John Q. Kim ***New!*** *[Keyboard your name, too, so anyone can read it.]*

►**Enclosure: Resume** ***New!***

►***ADD New, improved statistics, on ONE LINE—but only for this assignment, not for your REAL job application letters. Your statistics are a tool to help YOU!***

Words 253; s/p 2.0, w/s 8.7; passives 0%, Reading ease 67.9, Grade level 5.9

J.A.L. Content & Stats (V-16) *Technical Writing, An Introduction* *2009.9 (2007) © mns*

DRESS UP YOUR LETTER

Letterhead, Page Border, Color & Paper

Now the contents of your letter are organized and complete. But our job's not done yet!

You may want to "dress up" your letter with a **page border** a **letterhead**, or both.

LETTERHEAD

• Let's make a **CCCI Letterhead**, for a more professional appearance.

Center Your Name.

Make it BIG & Bold.

Put your **C**omplete, **C**orrect **C**ontact **I**nformation in your Letterhead. Line it up neatly.

Balance the page, left to right. Use your **CENTERING** button on the toolbar, **not** "Tab".

Make sure your FONT is big enough and clear enough for a manager (40+) to read.

Check your letterhead by eye for ACCURACY. Spell-check it, too!

Ask another person for their opinion. "How does it look?" They can be very helpful.

PAGE BORDER

• Make borders on the Format menu. See next page for detailed instructions.

Don't make your border too black and thick, unless it's a funeral announcement.

Examples follow, but only in Black and White.

Use your imagination. Your letter represents you. But keep it conservative and business-like, unless you're applying to be a fashion designer!

ADD A COLOR

• You could add **ONE dark ink color** to your letterhead or page border, or both.

• PAPER

You can choose **high quality, pale-colored paper** to add a special, personal touch.

Statistics (V-6): Words 216; s/p 1.5, w /sentence 8.0; passives 4%, Reading Ease 71.8, Grade Level 5.2

Dress Up Your J.A.L. *Technical Writing, An Introduction* *2009.11, 2009.3 © mns*

FMPG

Farm Machinery Promotion Group
School of Mechanical Engineering
Yeungnam University

Lab 4XX, 214-1 Dae-dong,
Gyeongsan City, Gyeongbuk
Republic of Korea 712-749

Phone: 82-53-7777-8888
Fax: 82-53-7777-8890
E-mail: student@naver.net

Your Name Bold

YOUR HOME ADDRESS
214-1 Dae-Dong, Gyeongsan
Gyeongbuk, Korea 712-749

[Contact info must be correct, complete, readable and well lined-up.]

Home: (053) 215-TTYY
Mobile: 010-6000-XXXX
E-mail: goodframe@naver.com

HOW TO SET MARGINS & PAGE BORDER

Here are some "technical" writing tips for using Microsoft Word 2003. To find the same functions in Word 2007, consult "Help" - blue circle, white question mark.

PAGE MARGINS

To set the page margins, go to the File menu. Go down to 페이지설정 (U). Adjust the settings & click OK.

The margin settings on this page are: Top 3.0 cm Bottom 3.0 cm Left 3.0 cm Right 3.0 cm

To set the page margins as a default, go to the File menu. Go down to 페이지설정 (U). Adjust the settings & click 기본값 (D) for Default.

PAGE BORDER

To put a border on a page, go to the Format menu, 서식. Click 테두리 or (B) for Borders (& Shading). Click the Page Border tab at the top. Then select the Setting, Style, Color and Width of line you prefer. Keep it simple!

At right, in Preview, click the "border" boxes. The little diagram shows the result. To confirm your choice, click OK.

To move the border relative to page edge, or relative to the text (as on this page), click **options** button in Preview, and increase or decrease the distance. This can solve the problem of a border not printing.

MAKING A BOX

To make a box around a word, phrase or paragraph, highlight the text you want inside the box. Go to the Format menu, and click Borders and Shading. At right, in Preview, click any "border" box. The diagram will show a box. Click OK.

Statistics (V-23): words 211; s/p 2.5, w/s 9.9; passives 0%, Reading Ease 80.9, Grade Level 4.4

Set Margins & Page Border *Technical Writing, An Introduction* *(Rev.) Orig. 2009.2, mns*

JOB APPLICATIONS: READER'S QUESTIONS & WRITER'S ANSWERS

You will NOT be present when the company receives your application.
Your letter and resume must "speak" for themselves.

Do NOT expect the first reception to be friendly. Expect the people to be busy, stressed, overworked, impatient and not very receptive to your papers at all.

Your letter must get past the lowest level worker, who often does the first screening. WHAT JOB DO YOU WANT? ARE YOU QUALIFIED? These are the first questions. For any job, there are simply 2 piles: "Maybe" and "휴지통". This is the reality. Will your letter pass a first screening? And a second? OK.

Now "the boss" gets your package. He also has some questions:

Reader's Questions	**Your Letter Answers**
•What is THIS?	It's my Application Package.
•Who are you? (Oh, nice Letterhead!)	Here's my name, on the Letterhead.
•Is this addressed to me?	Dear Design Manager:
•What do you want? Why are you writing?	I am applying for _______ position.
•Why am I reading this?	Your AD asked me to apply to you.
•Why should I consider YOU?	Because I am qualified.
•What do you know about this company?	I have visited your Website.
•Do you have a resume?	My resume is attached.
•Do I want to talk to this person?	Please invite me for an interview.
•Where and how can I reach you?	Full contact info is on my letterhead.
•Do you have normal business manners?	This letter begins and ends politely.
•What's your name, again?	I've printed and signed my full name.

Statistics: Words 245; Avgs: s/p 2.5, w/s 5.9; Readability: passives 5%, FRE 83.2, GL 3.1

Job Application / Cover Letters *Technical Writing, An Introduction* *(Rev. 8) 10 Oct 08 © mns*

LETTER SLOTS

Preparing to Send Your Job Application

CHECK these LETTER "SLOTS" BEFORE you send out your application:

S TAPLE	**Staple your pages together.** **Insert <u>one</u> staple in top left corner.** **A staple turns your pages into a package.**
L ETTER	**Letter goes on top. Lead with your letter.** **Let's advertise! "Read me first!"** **Letter introduces you and your resumé.**
O N	**Only good applicants get interviews.** **Open doors with a good application letter.**
T OP	**Top two reasons we call this a "Cover" Letter:** **First, it physically COVERS the other pages.** **Second, it SUMMARIZES (and so, "covers")** **the high points of the Résumé.**
S IGN	**Sign the letter. Sign by hand, in ink.** **Signing personalizes your letter. Signing says you take legal responsibility for the written content.**
<u>PLUS +</u> SPELL CHECK & STATISTICS	**Spell check and Grammar check your letter.** **We ADD "readability statistics" during our course, to show that you've <u>used</u> the Spelling and Grammar Check Tools, AND that you <u>know</u> the level of difficulty in understanding your writing.** **"Readability" here means "level of difficulty."**

Statistics (V-23): Words 170; s/p 1.2, w/s 6.0; passives 0%, FRE 61.2, FKGL 6.2

SLOTS: Prep. to Send App. *Technical Writing, An Introduction* *2009.8.24 © mns*

COVER LETTER for WIN-WIN JOB APPLICATIONS

A Good Cover Letter Will:

1) Make a good first impression.
2) Address the reader's needs.
3) Introduce the sender.
4) Promote, market, advertise and sell the applicant's job-related skills.
5) Demonstrate, or show, the writer's letter-writing skills.
6) Introduce the resume.
7) Gain an invitation to an interview.
8) Provide good contact information.
9) Provide a record of the job application.
10) Provide talking points for the interview.

Statistics: Words 65; w/s 5.4; passives 0%, Flesch Reading Ease 47.8, Grade Level 7.9

Checklist for Grading Your Letter

(What I look for)

Letterhead

1. Readable, complete, well-aligned, balanced L↔R (Pleasing to the eye is also nice.)

Body

2. Recent Date, in one of 3 standard forms; receiver's mailing address, written in full
3. **TOPIC, bold and centered:** here, **Competition #** *(here* = your *Class # + Student #)* PLUS, **Title of Job you're applying for** or **"Letter of Self Introduction"**
4. Formal greeting and correct punctuation
5. **Say why you are writing,** preferably in sentence one, line one!
6. Supporting information & promotion of main idea—one to 5 paragraphs on one page
7. Formal "sign-off," with a comma
8. *Signature by hand, in black ink* - with name clearly typed, below
9. Enclosure: Resume *[Or, give a full list: resume, transcripts…]*
10. Reasonable, credible Readability statistics, presented on one line, at page bottom.

Statistics: Words 112; w/s 10.3; passives 0%, Flesch Reading Ease 46.2, Grade Level 9.3

G.C.L. & Checklist *Technical Writing, An Introduction* *(V-09.11) 20/02/08 © mns*

☎ Model Job Application Letters ☎

from

Technical Writing Course Graduates

SON DONG HO

164-12, Gamsam-Dong,
Dalseo-gu, Daegu,
South Korea 704-150

Home:(053)562-1182
Mobile: 010-4522-1182
E-mail: hefaitos@naver.com

June 24, 2009

Mr. Ha Dong Won
Human Resource Head Manager
Doosan Engine Head Office
69-3, Sinchon-Dong, Changwon-City
Gyeongnam, South Korea 641-370

Competition # 1199-20411685
Design Department

Dear Mr. Ha,

I am applying for the position of Design Engineer at Doosan Engine Co. I am happy to see the advertisement on your web site.

I major in Mechanical Engineering in Yeungnam University. I will graduate in February 2010. There are three reasons why I am a qualified applicant for the position:

First, I am able to use CATIA V5 very well. I can easily learn and use any other computer design tools. It means that you don't need to invest too much time in educating me.

Next, I study English every day in order to prepare to work with foreign co-workers. Now I am good at speaking English without studying abroad.

Third, I have experience in successfully finishing a project with LG Display Co. My team won the third prize among 10 teams. At that time, I was a team leader.

Thank you for reviewing my resume. I am heartily looking forward to your response about an interview for the position.

Sincerely yours,

Dongho Son

Enclosure: Resume
Statistics: Words 219; w/s 10.5; passive 0%, Reading Ease 57.7, Grade Level 7.8

Liu Wu-yao

Digital Media Technology

712-749
YeungnamUniversity, 214-1Dae-dong,
Gyeongsan, Gyeongbuk 712-749, Republic of Korea

Home Phone: 86)738-8281628
Mobile: 10-2232-2468
Email: vivy-liu@hotmail.com

October 5th, 2008

Mr. John A. Lasseter
Chief Creative Officer, Pixar and Disney Animation Studios
Pixar Animation Studios Inc.
1200 Park Ave.
Emeryville, CA 94608

Class#0210-20830053
Animation Department

Dear Mr. Lasseter:

I am applying for the position of animator at Pixar Animation Studio Inc. which you advertised on September 20, 2008.

I have not only taken most Digital Media courses offered at Huazhong Normal University but also lots of Animation programs classes outside school such as Maya, Flash, and CAD.

In addition, I am really absorbed in Animation. In order to follow my dream, I have changed major from Math Department at University. As a result, I gained the ability in Structure which is good for animation. Also I have worked a part-time job at an Advertising Company. Also, I have assisted in an animation program in school and now have had a program with 2 partners. I am looking forward to applying this experience at Pixar Animation Studios.

Thank you for taking time to review my resume. I would appreciate an opportunity to meet with you at an interview.

I look forward to meeting you.

Sincerely yours,

刘 炜 瑶

Wuyao Liu

Enclosure: Resume

Statistics: 160; w/s11.4; Readability: passives 0%, Reading ease 60.5, Grade level 10.8

Yu Lili

E-501-3,214-1 Dae-Dong,
Gyeongson City,Gyeongbuk,
Republic of Korea 712-749

Home:(053)810-8270
Mobile:010-7680-1988
E-mail:183579822@qq.com

October 7th, 2008

Mr. Song
Market Manager
Shandong International Trade Company
245 Street of Jinan City， Shandong Province
China 650301

Competition # 0210-20830091
Letter of Application for Merchandiser

Dear Mr. Song:

I am applying for the position of merchandiser in your company which you have advertised on the Internet on Tuesday, October 1, 2008.

I have the bachelor's degree from International Trade of Yunnan University, including three years' scholarships. I took certificates about merchandiser, IELTS and Japanese testamur 1 certificates.

In addition, I am especially interested in this position because I have work experience as a merchandiser in Oscer company in Kunming during 2005 and 2006.What's more I have one outstanding performance, and I really know how to cooperate with team players.

Thank you for taking your time to review my resume. I would appreciate the opportunity to discuss my qualifications more fully in a interview. I look forward to meeting you.

Sincerely yours,

Yu Lili

Yu Lili

Enclosure: Resume

(Statistics: Words 176; w/s 14.0; Readability: passives 0%, Reading Ease 33.4, Grade level 12.8)

Kim Kang Min

380-4 Sungdang 1Dong	Phone: 053) 621-1355
Dalseo-Gu Daegu	Cell Phone: 010-7727-4936
Korea 704-080	Email: knightkg@naver.com

May 24, 2009

Mr. Mun Jun Whan
Hyundai Motor Company 231 Yangje-Dong
Seoul Seocho-Gu South Korea 137-938

Competition #1163-20411565
Researcher of Automobile Department

Dear Mr. Jung:

I am applying for the position of researcher of automobile department in your company. I found your advertisement on your website on Saturday April 4, 2009.

I will graduate from YEUNGNAM University in February 2011, with major in automotive frame design using MS Office, C++, CAD, CAM, Catia and working model.

I would like to contribute to research the new generation of Hydrogen Automobile that Hyundai motors plans to produce beginning 2012.

Thank you for taking your time to review my resume. I would be happy to show you my research portfolio at an interview. I really want to show you my ability for this position. References are available on request. I look forward to your positive response and I hope to meet you soon.

Sincerely yours,

김강민

KANG-MIN KIM

Enclosure: Resume

Statistics: words 160; w/s 10.7; Readability : passives 0%, Reading ease 61.4, Grade Level 8.0

KIM, JEONG-HYUN
Mechanical Engineering

302 /1302, Daerim Hansup Town
Yeonil-eup, Nam-gu, Pohang-si
Gyeongbuk, Korea 790-754

Home: (054) 278 2874
Mobile: 010 6808 7151
E-mail: davidkim@ynu.ac.kr

November 11, 2008

Mr. KIM, MOO SANG
Human Resource Head Manager
Hyundai Kia Motors Namyang Institute
Jangdeok-dong, Hwaseong-si
Gyeonggi-do, Korea 445-706

Competition # 0685 - 20746084
Functional Test Team

Dear Mr. Kim:

I am applying for the position on the Functional Test Team in Hyundai Kia Motors, Namyang Institute. I found the advertisement on your website.

I will graduate from Yeungnam University in 2009. My major is mechanical engineering. I carried out aerodynamic study about rear shape and rear view mirror of the vehicle. I had great opportunities to present some results about rear view mirror in conferences. In addition, I won the competition organized by my school through the results. My school funded me to visit other laboratory due to rewards. I visited vehicle aerodynamic laboratory of Royal Melbourne Institute Technology (RMIT) in Melbourne.

I have experience with experimental tools. Those are Hot-Wire, Laser Doppler Velocimetry (LDV) and Particle Image Velocimetry (PIV). I am talented to analyze turbulent signal and spectrum by using the hot-wire system. In addition, I am skilled to conduct digital signal processing as handling MATLAB and C++.

I hope you will invite me for an interview. Thank you in advance for your consideration.

Sincerely yours,

김 정 현

JEONG-HYUN KIM

Enclosure: Resume

[Statistics: Words 242; w/s 11.0; Readability: passive 0%, Reading Ease 35.5, Grade Level 11.0]

Tran Viet Hong

214-1 Dae-dong Gyeongsan-si Gyeongsangbuk-do
Yeungnam University Dormitory, Room A109

010-7909-7219
tvhong@gmail.com

November 25, 2008

Prof. Michael Neil Shapiro
Associate Foreign Professor
School of Mech. Eng., Yeungnam University
214-1 Dae-dong Gyeongsan-si Gyeongsangbuk-do
712-749

Competition # 0685-20750092
Teaching Department

Dear Prof. Shapiro,

I am applying for the position of Teaching Assistant in Technical Writing course at School of Mechanical Engineering, Yeungnam University as advertised on Yeungnam University's homepage on September 15, 2008.

I meet all your requirements on English proficiency and experience:

- TOEFL and TOEIC scores are greater than 650 and 900, respectively.
- Three months experience teaching English in China.

Moreover, I have been in Korea for 4 years and now am on PhD course here. So, I am familiar with the Korean education system and the circumstance at Yeungnam University. I will come back to teaching job at my university in Vietnam when I finish the degree. I am looking forward to applying my knowledge and developing my career. In addition, my computer skill is very good. It will help in preparing materials for lectures.

Thank you for taking your time to review my resume. I desire to take this chance. Hence, I will make myself available at your convenience for an interview.

I look forward to meeting you.

Sincerely yours,

Tran Viet Hong

Enclosure: Resume

Statistics: words 211; s/p 2.1; w/s 12.1; Readability: passives 0%, Reading Ease 51.0, Grade Level 9.1.

Isabelle Nguyen

Yeungnam University Dormitory I 423,
214-1 Dae-Dong, Gyeongsan, Gyeongbuk 712-749,
Republic of Korea

Mobile Phone: 010-5807-1704
Email: isabelle.nguyen1@etu.u-cergy.fr

November 12th, 2008

Mr. Hwang Min Lee
Human Resource Head Manager
Deloitte
7th Fl., Sungan Gwangjang Officetel
87-36 Dooryu2-dong, Dalseo-gu 704-908

Competition # 0210-20830117
Accounting Department

Dear Mr. Lee:

I am applying for an internship as a General Accountant at a Korean Deloitte Office, as your French co-worker Denise Roupion advised me to do after my summer-job at Deloitte France.

I graduated first of my class as an undergraduate in Economics & English. Since then, I have taken most of Accounting and Management courses offered by both University of Cergy-Pontoise (France) and Yeungnam University. I have always endeavored to do my best and aimed at excellence.

Moreover, my experiences as an Accountant for BNP Paribas and Deloitte during summer holidays have given me precious knowledge about the professional accounting environment. I am hardworking, open minded and always willing to learn more, which are essential qualities to succeed in this job.

I would be grateful if you could take my application into consideration, and happier if you could contact me for an interview.

I thank you for your attention and look forward to hearing from you soon.

Sincerely yours,

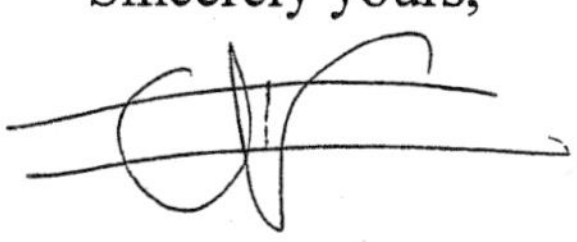

Isabelle Nguyen.

Stat : words 210; w/s 18.6; Readability: passives 0%, Reading Ease 59.4, Grade Level 9.6

Hong Sung Chul

308-102, Jigok Green Villa
Jigok-dong, Namgu, Pohang,
Gyeonkbuk, Korea 790-751

Home Phone: (054)221-0328
Mobile: 017-521-6316
E-mail: schong1@postown.net

November 14, 2009

Mr. Lee

Human Resource Team Manager, POSCO

1, Goedong-dong, Nam-gu, Pohang, Gyeongbuk

Korea 790-300, Pohang P.O.Box 36

Competition # 0628 – 20850073

Rolling Technology Research Group

Dear Mr. Lee,

I am applying for the position in the Rolling Technology Research Group in your company that you have advertised on your company website.

I have a master's degree in mechanical engineering from Korea Advanced Institute of Science and Technology. I am now pursuing a doctorate in the School of Electrical Engineering at Yeungnam University.

In addition, I have performed 15 projects related to rolling process control technology since 1991. I can handle several program languages such as MATLAB and C for developing process control programs.

Thank you for reviewing my resume. I hope to get the opportunity to tell my qualifications fully in an interview. I look forward to meeting you.

Sincerely yours,

Hong Sung Chul

Hong Sung Chul

Enclosure: Resume

Statistics (except Letterhead): Words 148; w/s 13.8; Readability: passive 0%, Reading Ease 40.3, Grade level 11.0

"Why writing a job application letter
is not a useful task for me now"

by

Two Chunma Honors Freshmen

Why writing a job application letter is not useful task for me now.

Han-sol, Jang, Class #3159

I tried to write a job application letter, but I do not have lots of experiences. So it was really hard work for me. Then, I decided to write why writing a job application letter is not that useful work for me now. There are 3 reasons that writing a job application letter is useless for me in this moment. I'm just freshman and I won't apply ordinary company. Also, there are some agencies which write job application letter and job application instead of their clients. And, I will write a little bit more specific about those reasons.

First reason that I don't want to learn how to write cover letter is that I'm only first grade student now. So I think I could spend more time learning other things. May be I can study my major or some professional things. Also, even if I learn how to write cover letter, nobody can be sure that I will remember the way to write it. I will start to get a job at least 3 years later, and I don't think I can remember every skill. May be I have to study everything again, and that is just waste of time. Thus, I disagree with writing job application letter now.

Second, I will not join an ordinary company. I will pass CPA (Certified Public Accountant) or be a judicial officer. And, usually in Korea, those kinds of firms do not accept job application letter. So I don't think I must know a lot about cover letters. And I will not apply for the company which requires English application letter. I will stay in Korea. So I don't think learning about cover letter in English very good idea. I perhaps have to learn how to write it in Korean again later. That is just extravagancy in both effort and time. And I think this explains why I think writing a job application letter is not useful exercise for me now.

The last reason that I don't think writing a job application letter is an important exercise is I know there are some agencies for job application letter. I never used one of them, but I surely know there are many professional writers who write job application letters. They not only write job application letters but also other documents that people have to hand in for their job. And I think their writing is much better than my writing. Probably their application letter would work better than my letter because their letter seems much more professional and cleaned up. Lots of job seekers ask those agencies. I think they do because that is much more efficient. I don't have to spend too much time on it. If I don't have to write a job application letter later, why should I have to learn?

I mentioned three reasons. It is too early to learn how to write a cover letter for me and I do not think I will use that skill. Also, I can ask some professionals to write it instead of me. May be those statements seems like my self-justification, but I will say again that writing a job application letter is really not useful task for me now.

[Statistics: Words 554; s/p 6.3, w/s 14.4; passives 0%, Reading ease 70.0, Grade level 7.0]

Lee Ji Hye

I'm writing this essay to explain the reason why I didn't write a job application letter.

Your English class is very useful and interesting to me especially because you teach what is essential but other teachers don't usually teach. I think writing a resume and a job application letter is also a great activity. Almost everybody will do it at least once in a lifetime. Since I think like this, I looked for some companies to apply for (e.g. KB financial group, Samsung SDS, Hyundai motor company, etc.) But after I started writing a job application letter, I realized that I'm not ready to do this. I want to work for a finance division but I have little experience on that. Actually I have nothing to write about that. I even haven't learned anything about the science of finance. If I send my worthless letter to a head manager, I will never be taken into that company! He/ She will laugh at my resume (What is this girl thinking she's going to do?). Some students made up their story or experience but I don't think it is the right thing. It's just their dream, not reality. Companies need real people, not imaginary people. Of course it's possible for them to become like that or better than that. However, even if saying that they have a possibility can be a help, possibility without ability will sound hollow in the actual workplace.

I think writing a resume in this course should be a serious job. This course is generally for the 3rd or 4th grade students who 'should' find their job sooner or later. Those students will learn a lot in this course and the resumes they write will probably be used for their real application for employment. Because of this usefulness, they will do their best. It will be great if I can have the same passion about writing this, but I can't. Though I looked for some companies to apply for, it doesn't mean that I will really do it later. Actually, I'm preparing for the test to enter public service. After getting through two exams, I will be a civil servant. There is no need to write a resume. Though I don't think I will work as a civil servant for my lifetime (It's too boring, isn't it?), I will at least have much more experience to write on my resume to enter a private company by then. It will be a very different resume from what I can write now.

Writing a resume (what *[as]* we did before) was not easy, but I think it's easier than writing a job application letter. I came to realize that I lack many things. I have to be more modest like the root of plant which always places itself in the low place. But that's why it can absorb various nutrients and grow big. I'm still a freshman. I'm an unfinished work and I have to fill myself ceaselessly. I think it will be successful if I make an effort as if I fill my resume.

[Statistics: Words 515; s/p 8.5, w/s 15.1; passives 5% FRE 71.5, FKGL 7.0]

PART 8 - WRITING A GENERAL BUSINESS OR SALES LETTER

AIDA–"Four Letters That Sell" Or, Sequence of Letter Content
How To Write A Business Letter by Malcolm Forbes
◎ 업무용 편지 작성 요령
–Bilingual Version: English & Korean Together

A I D A*

"FOUR LETTERS THAT SELL"

Or, Sequence of Letter Content

Attention!

Catch the reader's <u>attention</u>.
If not, they will not READ your letter, or take in your information.
▷ Address the reader's main concern.

Interest!

Say something that <u>interests</u> the reader.
Give them a reason to keep reading.
▷ Facts & numbers are interesting.

Desire!

Offer the reader something he/she <u>wants</u>.
Fear and Desire are the strongest motivators.
▷ List benefits to the reader.

Action!

Tell the reader HOW they can GET what they want. Or, AVOID what they don't want.

▷ Call for <u>action</u>:
What should they <u>DO</u> now?

*AIDA is a well-known strategy, model or writing plan for business letters.

Search the Web—you'll see!

Can you hear the *Triumphal March* from ***AIDA***? It's music to my ears!

Statistics: Words 115; Avgs: s/p 1.5, w/s 4.9; Readability: passives 0%, Reading Ease 76.9, Grade Level 3.7

Letters, AIDA (V-15) *Technical Writing, An Introduction* *2009.02 (2008) © mns*

How To Write A Business Letter
By Malcolm Forbes

업무용 편지 작성 요령 (Malcolm Forbes)

A good business letter can get you a job interview, get you off the hook, or get you money. It's totally asinine to blow your chances of getting whatever you want with a business letter that turns people off instead of turning them on. The best place to learn to write is in school. If you're still there, pick your teachers' brains. If not, big deal. I learned to ride a motorcycle at 50 and fly balloons at 52. It's never too late to learn.

잘 쓰여진 업무용 편지는 취업 면접 기회를 가져다 줄 수도 있고, 위기 상황에서 벗어 나게 할 수 있게 해주거나 돈도 벌 수 있게 해줄 수 있다. 흥미를 끌어야 할 때 오히려 흥미를 잃게 만드는 편지를 써서 원하는 것을 다 얻을 수 있는 절호의 기회를 날리는 것이야 말로 참으로 어리석은 짓일 것이다. 글쓰기를 배우기 가장 좋은 장소는 학교이다. 만약 당신이 아직 학교에 있다면, 학교 선생님 머리 속에 든 지혜를 빌려라. 만약 학교에 있지 않다고 해도 대단할 것 없다. 나는 50 세에 오토바이 타는 것을 배웠고, 52 세에 기구를 타는 법을 배웠다. 배우는데 있어서 너무 늦다는 것은 있을 수 없다.

Over 10,000 business letters come across my desk every year. They seem to fall into three categories: stultifying if not stupid, mundane (most of them), and first rate (rare). Here's the approach I've found that separates the winners from the losers--it starts before you write your letter:

매년 10,000 개 이상의 업무용 편지가 내 책상으로 온다. 그것들은 대개 3 가지 부류에 속하는 것 같다. 멍청하기까지는 아니어도 지루한 것들, 그저 그런 것 (대부분), 아주 훌륭한 것 (드물게)등 이다. 내 경험에 의해 볼 때 승자와 패자를 가를 정도로 중요한 접근 법이 있는데 이것은 편지를 쓰기 이전에 이미 시작된다.

<u>Know what you want:</u>
<u>네가 원하는 것이 무엇인지 알아라</u>

If you don't, write it down--in one sentence. "I want to get an interview within the next two weeks." Then, list the major points you want to get across--it'll keep you on course. If you're answering a letter, check the points that need answering and keep the letter in front of you while you write. This way you won't forget anything--that would cause another round of letters. For goodness' sake, answer promptly if you're going to answer at all. Don't sit on a letter--that invites the person on the other end to sit on whatever you want in return.

원하는 것이 무엇인지 모른다면, 우선 그것을 한 문장으로 적어보아라. “ 나는 앞으로 2 주 내에 인터뷰 기회를 가지고 싶다.” 그런 후, 독자에게 전달하고 싶은 주요 사항들을 나열해보라. 그것이 주제에서 이탈하는 것을 막아줄 것이다. 만약 다른 사람의 편지에 대한 답장을 쓰고 있다면 대답할 필요가 있는 요점들을 점검하고 답장을 쓰는 동안 내내 편지를 늘 가까이 두고 있어야 한다. 이렇게 하면 대답하는 것을 깜빡 하는 바람에 자칫 한 번 더 편지가 오고 가야 하는 는 것을 막을 수 있다. 또한 이왕 답할 요량이면 제발 신속하게 회답하라. 답장을 질질 끌면 편지를 보낸 상대방도 당신이 보낼 답장 내용에 속절없이 매일 수 밖에 없게 만들고 만다.

Plunge right in:
곧장 본론으로 들어 가라.

Call the reader by name--"Dear Mr. Chrisanthopoulos" not "Dear Sir, Madam, or Ms."--and be sure to spell it right. That'll get him (thus, you) off to a good start. (Usually, you can get the name just by phoning the company--or from a business directory in your nearest library.)

읽는 사람의 이름을 직접 호명하라. – 친애하는 선생님 또는 부인하는 투가 아니라 친애하는 Chrisanthopoulos 씨와 같이 부르고 철자를 틀리지 않도록 주의하라. 이렇게 하는 것이 읽는 사람이 (그리고 당신 또한) 상큼한 기분으로 출발할 수 있게 만들 것이다. (통상적으로 회사에 전화를 걸어나 가까운 도서관에 있는 주소록 등을 통하여 사람들의 이름을 알아낼 수 있다.)

Tell what your letter is about in the first paragraph using one or two sentences. Don't keep your readers guessing or they might discard your letter--even before they finish it. People who read business letters are as human as you and I. Reading a letter shouldn't be a chore, reward readers for the time they give you.

첫 번째 문단에서 한 두 문장으로 편지가 무엇에 대한 것인지 쓰라. 읽는 사람이 편지의 내용을 뭘까 하고 계속 궁금해 하면서 읽어 가도록 만들지 마라. 아마도 편지를 다 읽기도 전에 내 던져 버릴 지도 모른다. 업무용 편지를 읽는 사람들도 당신이나 나처럼 인간이기 때문에 편지를 읽는 것이 귀찮은 일이 되지 않도록 배려해야 하고, 읽는 사람이 할애한 시간에 대한 보답하도록 노력해야 한다.

Write so readers enjoy it:
상대방이 읽는 것을 즐길 수 있도록 써라.

- **Write the entire letter from the reader's point of view**. What's in it for the reader? Beat the reader to the draw by answering the questions and objections that might arise.

  편지 전체를 독자들의 입장에서 생각하여 작성하라. 상대방을 위해 무엇을 편지에 담았는가? 발생 가능한 질문이나 반론에 대하여 미리 답해 둠으로써 상대방보다 앞서 나가도록 하라.

- **Be positive**. The reader will be more receptive to what you have to say.

  긍정적으로 쓰라. 그러면 상대도 당신이 말해야 하는 내용에 더욱 잘 수긍할 것이다.

- **Be nice**. Contrary to the cliché, genuinely nice guys most often finish first or very near it. I admit it's not easy when you've got a gripe. To be agreeable while disagreeing--that's an art.

  친절 하라. 속설과는 반대로, 진정한 의미로 선한 사람들이 승리하거나 그것에 가까이 갈 경우가 많은 것이다. 불만이 있을 때 친절하기 쉽지 않다는 것은 인정하지만 서로 다른 의견을 가지고 있으면서도 합의할 수 있는 것이야 말로 대화의 기술이다.

- **Be natural**. Write the way you talk. Imagine the reader sitting in front of you--what would you say? Business jargon too often is cold, stiff, and unnatural. Suppose I came up to you and said, "I acknowledge receipt of your letter and I thank you." You'd think, "Huh? You're putting me on."

  자연스럽게 하라. 말을 하는 것처럼 글을 써라. 독자가 앞에 앉아 있다고 상상할 때 뭐라고 말하겠는가? 업무용 전문 용어는 종종 너무 차갑고, 딱딱하고, 부자연스럽다. 당신에게 다가가서 "나는 당신의 편지를 받은 것을 정식 인정한다. 감사한다." 라는 식으로 어색하게 말한다면 당신은 아마도 "허? 날 놀리고 있군." 이라고 생각할 것이다.

- **The acid test**--read your letter out loud when you're done. You might get a shock--but you'll know for sure if it sounds natural. *[Emphasis added, mns]*

  실증 테스트 - 편지를 다 쓰고 난 뒤 큰소리로 읽어보라. 무슨 뚱딴지 같은 소리냐고 충격적으로 받아들일지는 몰라도 이렇게 해보면 편지가 자연스러운지 아닌지 알게 될 것이다.

- **Don't be cute or flippant.** The reader won't take you seriously. This doesn't mean you've got to be dull. You prefer your letter to knock 'em dead rather than bore 'em to death.

  너무 앙증맞게 또는 경박스럽게 쓰지 마라. 아마도 독자는 당신을 진지한 사람으로 보지 않을 것이다. 그렇다고 지루하게 써야 한다는 말이 아니다. 당신의 편지에 지루해 죽게 만드는 것보다는 재미있어 죽게 만드는 편이 낫다.

In your communication:
서신에서:

1. **Have a sense of humor.** That's refreshing anywhere--a nice surprise in a business letter.

   유머 감각을 가져라. 유머는 어디에서든지 새로움을 느끼게 해준다 – 업무용 편지에서 신선한 충격을 선사할 것이다.

2. **Be specific.** If I tell you there's a new fuel that could save gasoline, you might not believe me. But suppose I tell you this: "Gasohol"--10% alcohol, 90% gasoline--works as well as straight gasoline. Since you can make alcohol from grain or corn stalks, wood or wood waste, coal--even garbage, it's worth some real follow-through. Now you've got something to sink your teeth into.

   구체적으로 써라. 만약 내가 가솔린을 절약할 수 있는 새로운 연료가 있다고 한다면, 당신은 그냥 날 믿지는 않을 것이다. 하지만, "가소올"– 10% 알코올, 90% 가솔린— 일반 가솔린만큼 좋습니다. 곡물, 옥수수 줄기, 나무 또는 나무 쓰레기, 석탄— 심지어 쓰레기로부터 알코올로 만들 수 있기 때문에, 한 번 써 보실 만 할 거라고 권하면 당신도 관심을 갖고 달려들게 될 것이다.

3. **Lean heavier on nouns and verbs, lighter on adjectives. Use the active voice instead of the passive.** Your writing will have more guts. Which of these is stronger? Active voice: "I kicked out my money manager." Or, passive voice: "My money manager was kicked out by me." (By the way, neither is true. My son, Malcolm Jr., manages Forbes' money--he's a brilliant moneyman.)

   명사나 동사에 더 많은 중점을 두고, 형용사에는 적게 써라. 수동태 보다는 능동태를 사용하라. 글이 더욱 힘있어 질 것이다. 다음 중에 어느 것이 더 힘 있는 메시지를 전달하겠는가? 능동태: " 나는 내 자금관리인을 해고했다," 수동태: " 내 자금 관리인은 나에 의해 해고당했다". (그건 그렇고, 실제 상황은 이것도 저것도 아니다. 내 아들 말콤 주니어는 아주 영리한 자금 관리인이라서 Forbes 의 돈을 아직도 굳건히 관리하고 있다.)

<u>Give it the best you've got:</u>
<u>**최선을 다해 쓰라.**</u>

When you don't want something enough to make the effort, making an effort is a waste. To make the effort:
충분한 노력을 경주할 만한 그 무엇인가를 원하고 있는 않다면 수고 자체가 낭비가 된다. 노력을 경주하려면:

- **Make your letter look appetizing** -- or you'll strike out before you even get to bat. Type it on good-quality [standard, A4] stationery. Keep it neat. Use paragraphing that makes it easier to read.

  편지를 읽을 구미가 당기도록 써라 --- 그렇지 않고서는 당신은 야구방망이를 잡아 보기도 전에 스트라이크 아웃을 당할 것이다. 양질의 종이 (정식 A4 용지) 위에 깔끔하게 타이프 쳐라. 읽기 쉽도록 문단을 나누어라.

- **Keep your letter short** -- to one page, if possible. Keep your paragraphs short. After all, who's going to benefit if your letter is quick and easy to read? You. For emphasis, <u>*underline*</u> important words.

  편지를 짧게 쓰라—가능하다면 한 페이지로. 문장을 간결하게 만들어라. 편지를 빠르고 쉽게 읽을 수 있도록 쓰여졌다면 누구에게 이익이 돌아오겠는가? 바로 당신이다. 강조해야 할 때는 중요한 단어에 밑줄을 그어라.

- **Make it perfect.** No typos, no misspellings, no factual errors. If you're sloppy and let mistakes slip by, the person reading your letter will think you don't know better or don't care. Do you?

  완벽하게 만들어라. 오타나 틀린 철자, 사실적 오류 등이 없게 해라. 만약 편지가 단정하지 못하거나 실수를 간과한 채 보내면, 편지를 읽는 사람은 당신을 덜 떨어지거나 무관심한 인간으로 치부할 것이다. 당신은 그런 인간인가?

- **Be crystal clear.** You won't get what you're after if your reader doesn't get the message.

  내용을 극명하게 써라. 독자가 글의 의도를 알아내지 못하면 당신이 얻고자 하는 것을 결국 얻을 수 없게 될 것이다.

- **Use good English.** If you're still in school, take all the English and writing courses you can. The way you write and speak can really help--or hurt. If you're not in school (even if you are), get the little 71-page gem by Strunk & White, *Elements of Style*. It's in paperback. It's fun to read and loaded with tips on good English and good writing.

  훌륭한 영어를 사용해라. 아직도 학교에 다니고 있다면 들을 수 있는 모든 영어와 영작문 과목을 들어라. 당신이 글 쓰는 방식이나 말하는 방식은 매사에 도움이 되는지 해가 되는지 할 것이다. 만약 학교에 있지 않다면 (이점에서는 비록 학교에 다니고 있어도 마찬가지겠지만), Strunk & White 가 쓴 71 페이지짜리 명저, Elements of Style 을 구해서 읽어라. (값이 싼) 종이표지 본으로 읽기 재미있는데다 훌륭한 영어와 훌륭한 글쓰기에 대한 조언들이 가득하다.

- **Don't put on airs.** Pretense invariably impresses only the pretender.

  잘난 척 하지 마라. 가식은 언제나 가식자에게만 인상을 줄 수 있을 뿐이다.

- **Don't exaggerate.** Even once. Your reader will suspect everything else you write.

  과장하지 마라. 단 한번만이라고 과장하면 독자는 당신이 쓴 글들 모두를 의심할 것이다.

- **Distinguish opinions from facts.** Your opinions may be the best in the world. But opinions are not gospel. You owe it to your reader to identify *[distinguish]* opinions from facts. The dumbest people I know are those who "Know It All."

  주관적인 사견과 객관적 사실을 구분하라. 당신의 의견이 세상에서 제일 좋을 수도 물론 있지만 그것이 복음이 될 수는 없다. 독자에게 당신의 사견인 부분과 사실인 부분을 명확히 구분해줄 책임이 있다. 이 세상에서 가장 어리석은 사람은 자기가 모든 것을 다 안다고 치부하는 사람들이다.

- **Be honest.** It'll get you further in the long run. If you're not, you won't rest easy.

  진실하도록 하라. 장기적으로 볼 때 진실한 것이 더 효과가 있을 것이다. 누구나 진실하지 않으면 편히 쉴 수도 없을 것이다.

- **Edit ruthlessly.** Somebody has said that words are a lot like inflated money--the more words that you use, the less each one is worth. Right on. Go through your entire letter just as many times as it takes. Search out and annihilate all unnecessary words, and sentences--even entire paragraphs.

  철저하게 편집하라. 예전 누가 말했듯이 말이란 인플레 된 돈과 같다. – 말이 많으면 많을 수록 개개의 가치가 떨어지게 마련이다. 맞다! 편지 전체를 몇 번이 되든 반복해서 훑어 봐라. 불필요한 단어, 문장, 심지어 단락 전체 라 하지라도 모두 찾아서 제거해라.

Sum it up and get out:
요약과 마침

The last paragraph should tell the reader exactly what you want *the reader* to do--or what *you're* going to do. Keep it short and sweet. "May I have an appointment? Next Monday, May 16, I'll call your secretary to see when is convenient for you." Close with something simple like, "Sincerely." And for heaven's sake sign legibly. The biggest ego trip I know is a completely illegible signature. Good luck; I trust you will get what you're after!

마지막 단락에서는 당신이 독자에게 바라는 것 또는 당신이 하려고 하는 것을 명확하게 밝혀야 한다. 간결하고 상큼하게 써라. "다음주 월요일인 5 월 16 일에 약속을 해도 될까요? 편리하신 언제인지 비서에게 전화해서 알아 볼게요." 그리고 "Sincerely." 와 같은 간단한 말로 마무리 지어라. 그리고, 제발, 싸인 좀 알아 볼 수 있게 하라. 세상에서 가장 자기 중심적인 행위는 도통 알아 볼 수 없는 싸인을 하는 것이다. 여러분이 추구하는 것을 얻을 것으로 믿으며 행운을 빕니다.

MALCOLM FORBES

"Power of the Printed Word"
Adapted from thoughts of Malcolm Forbes,
Founder of *Forbes* Magazine

With permission:
International Paper Company

[Statistics (English): words 1133; s/p 4.6, w/s 9.7; Readability: passives 0%, Reading Ease 76.5, Grade Level 4.9]

Korean Translation by Shim Jae Sool & Alice Mira Chung; Editing & Streamlining by Chung Mo

PART 9 - TWO RADIO SCRIPTS
from
V.O.A. SPECIAL ENGLISH

V.O.A. Special English on Radio - What Makes Special English Special?

Engineers Without Borders (Transcript) - Engineering Low-Tech Solutions

► Questions on Engineers Without Borders

۞ 도움이 필요한 개발 도상국들을 위한 로우테크(low-tech) 해결 방안 설계

Past Tense Verbs - V.O.A. Wright Brothers, with Hints on Pronunciation

The Wright Brothers (Transcript)

► Powered Flight–In English! Simple calculations of time and distance

Teaching Points:

"If you draw it correctly on paper, it will be right when you build it."

Doing "simple" math calculations using input data in English

Special English on Radio

Every day, around the world, the Voice of America broadcasts news and feature programs in Special English. Click on the Frequencies link at the top of the right column to learn how to find us.

Three Elements Make Special English Unique

- It has a core vocabulary of 1500 words. Most are simple words that describe objects, actions or emotions. Some words are more difficult. They are used for reporting world events and describing discoveries in medicine and science.
- Special English writers use short, simple sentences that contain only one idea. They use active voice. They do not use idioms.
- Special English broadcasters read at a slower pace, about two-thirds the speed of standard English. This helps people learning English hear each word clearly. It also helps people who are fluent English speakers understand complex subjects.*

Each Special English broadcast is 30 minutes long. Most begin with world news, followed by a short report, then a 15 minute feature. Below is our daily schedule:

MONDAY	TUESDAY	WEDNESDAY	THURSDAY
Development Report	**Agriculture Report**	**Health Report**	**Education Report**
Issues that affect people in developing countries	*News about farming and food production*	*The latest research about diseases and medical advice*	*New developments in American education*
This is America	**Science in the News**	**Explorations**	**The Making of a Nation**
Traditions, ideas and life in the United States	*Reports about the latest scientific discoveries and medical news*	*Reports about outer space and the world around us*	*A series about the history of the United States*
FRIDAY	SATURDAY	SUNDAY	
Economics Report	**In the News**	**Words and Their Stories**	
News about business and finance in the U.S. and around the world	*In-depth reports about a person or event in the news*	*Features about American idioms and expressions*	
American Mosaic	**American Stories**	**People in America**	
A magazine show about popular culture and music	*Adaptations of short stories, children's books and original stories.*	*Biographies of influential Americans in history, politics, science, business, sports & entertainment*	

Source: www.voanews.com/specialenglish/radio_programs.cfm

* *Underline emphasis added, mns*

Engineering Low-Tech Solutions for Places in Need

Volunteers from a group called **Engineers Without Borders** are working on 300 projects in 45 countries.
Transcript of radio broadcast: 07 January 2008

MP3 - Download Audio
Listen to MP3
Listen in RealAudio

This is the VOA Special English Development Report.

Sometimes it takes an engineer to help a village. In poor communities, that help may come from volunteers with a group called Engineers Without Borders.

A civil engineering professor in the United States, Bernard Amadei, launched the group in two thousand. He did it with the help of his students and friends at the University of Colorado at Boulder.

Professor Amadei took a group of students to Belize to help build a water project. Since then, Engineers Without Borders has grown into an international nonprofit organization. Its budget last year was four million dollars. The group currently has about three hundred projects in forty-five countries.

Engineers Without Borders works on low-technology projects in mostly developing countries. In the Himalayan mountains of Nepal, for example, the group set up a sun-powered computer to communicate with a school in Kathmandu.

In Guatemala, volunteers have built ten bridges for communities cut off from nearby populations by seasonal rains. The group has built windmills in Kenya to improve crop production. And in Rwanda, Engineers Without Borders is rebuilding areas destroyed during the nineteen ninety-four genocide.

Cathy Leslie is the executive director of Engineers Without Borders. She tells us that many of the group's eight thousand members are students who volunteer as part of their college or university studies. Working professionals and retired engineers also have formed local chapters throughout the United States.

In the next five years, organizers hope more than ten percent of the members will be non-engineers. Cathy Leslie says community development involves not only engineering but many professions. She says it is equally important to help villages develop business plans and ways to finance and supervise projects.

Engineers Without Borders goes where it is invited. Communities can propose a project or seek assistance through one of its partners, such as Rotary International. Once a proposal is approved, student or professional chapters will compete for ownership of the project.

Local chapters are urged to work with a community for five to ten years. Individual chapters raise their own money for their projects.

And that's the VOA Special English Development Report, written by Jill Moss. For a link to Engineers Without Borders, go to voaspecialenglish.com. I'm Bob Doughty.

Statistics: Words 412; s/p 2.4 , w/s 13.4; passives 6%, Reading Ease 45.7, Grade Level 10.2

QUESTIONS ON ENGINEERS WITHOUT BORDERS – VOA REPORT

Class #________ Student #______________ Name ____________ Date ___.___.___

Instructions—Listen, read, then fill in the blanks:

1. Who started this organization, and when? A civil engineering professor,

______________ ____________ launched the group in ___________________.

2. What university did that professor and his students belong to?

They belonged to the University of __________________ at _________________.

3. How many projects does the group have currently? (#) They have about ___________________ (   ) projects in ________________ (   ) countries.

4. Briefly describe the group, “Engineers Without Borders”? *(See para. 4.)*

It's an ____.

5. What did they do in Nepal, and why? *(See paragraph 5.)*

They ____ to

____.

6. Very briefly, what have volunteers built in a) Guatemala and b) Kenya?

   a. They have __________ ________ ____________ for isolated communities.

   b. They have ___________ _______________ to ______________

   _________ _________________.

7. ___________ ____________ is the executive director.

8. The group has __________ _____________ members, including students.

   They hope that more than 10% will be non-________________.

9. What other kinds of professional help do villages need? *(Paragraph 8)*

They need help to _____________ ______________ plans, and ways to

_____________ and _______________ projects.

10. Local chapters usually work with communities for ________ to _______ years.

Statistics: Words 159; s/p 1.5, w/s 6.2; passives 0%, Reading Ease 70.8, Grade Level 4.9

Class Wk. EWB (Rev. 14, 1-ON)   Technical Writing   2009.8, 08.10 © Michael N. Shapiro

도움이 필요한 개발 도상국들을 위한 로우테크(low-tech) 해결 방안 설계

국경 없는 엔지니어들(Engineers Without Borders) 이라고 불리는 단체 소속의 봉사자들이 45 개 국가, 300 여 개의 프로젝트를 진행 중.
2008 년 1 월 7 일 라디오 방송 대본

MP3-오디오 다운받기
MP3 듣기
RealAudio 듣기

VOA 특별 영어 교육 보고서(Special English Development Report)입니다.

어떤 때는, 한 마을을 구원하기 위해 한 명의 엔지니어가 필요 할지도 모릅니다. 이 구원을 "국경 없는 엔지니어들" 이라고 불리는 단체의 봉사자들이 가난한 마을들에 가져다 줄지도 모르겠습니다.

미국의 한 토목과 교수, Bernard Amadei 교수가 2000 년도에 이 단체를 시작하였습니다. 콜로라도 주립 대학, Boulder 캠퍼스의 (University of Colorado at Boulder)학생들과 친구들의 도움으로 이루어진 일이었지요.

Amadei 교수는 한 그룹의 학생들을 수자원 프로젝트를 수행하기 위해 벨리즈로 데려갔었습니다. 이것이 시초가 되어 그 이후, 국경 없는 엔지니어들은 국제적인 비영리 단체로 발전하게 되었습니다. 작년(2007)의 예산액은 400 만 달러에 달했죠. 현재 이 단체는 45 개의 국가에서 300 여 개의 프로젝트를 진행 중입니다.

국경 없는 엔지니어들은 대부분 개발도상국에서 로우 테크(low-tech) 프로젝트들에 참여하고 있습니다. 예를 들어, 네팔의 히말라야 산맥에서 이들은 카트만두에 있는 학교와 통신하기 위해 태양에너지 컴퓨터를 설치했습니다.

과테말라에서 봉사자들은 우기에 주변 이웃들과 두절되고 마는 마을들을 위해 열 개의 다리들을 놓았습니다. 케냐에서는 농작물 수확량을 증진하기 위해 풍차를 세웠습니다. 그리고 르완다에서는, 1994 년도 대량학살에 의해 황폐화된 지역들을 재건설하고 있는 중입니다.

Cathy Leslie 는 국경 없는 엔지니어들의 상무이사입니다. 그녀에 의하면, 8 천명의 멤버 중 많은 이들이 전공 공부의 일부로 자원해 참여하는 대학생들이라고 합니다. 뿐만 아니라, 현직 전문 직업 종사자들과 은퇴한 엔지니어들 또한 전미 곳곳 지역본부(local chapters)를 구성해 활동하고 있습니다.

단체 운영자들은 앞으로 5 년 이내에 비(非)엔지니어멤버들이 10% 이상으로 증가하길 희망하고 있습니다. Cathy Leslie 는 마을 공동체 개발이 엔지니어들뿐만 아니라 많은 전문가들을 필요로 한다고 말합니다. 마을 공동체가 프로젝트를 위해 자금을 조달하고 하고 프로젝트를 감독하기 위해 사업 계획과 방법들을 개발하는 것을 돕는 것 또한 동등하게 중요한 일이라고 합니다.

국경 없는 엔지니어들은 초청받아 일을 하고 있습니다. 마을 공동체들은 프로젝트를 제안하거나 Rotary International 과 같은 국경 없는 엔지니어들의 많은 협력체 중 한 곳을 통해 도움을 요청할 수 있습니다. 제안안이 통과되면, 학생 혹은 전문가 본부(student or professional chapters)들이 프로젝트를 따기 위해 경쟁을 벌이게 됩니다.

국경 없는 엔지니어들은 지역본부(local chapters)들이 5 년에서 10 년 동안 한 마을과 일하는 것을 권장하고 있습니다. 각각의 지역본부들은 자신들의 프로젝트 자금을 스스로 모금하고 있습니다.

이상, Jill Moss 가 쓴 VOA 특별 영어 교육 보고서였습니다. 국경 없는 엔지니어들의 웹사이트 링크를 원하시면 voaspecialenglish.com 을 방문해 주십시오. 저는 Bob Doughty 였습니다. Translator, Alice Mira Chung, 정미라 역

Past Tense Verbs – V.O.A. Wright Brothers

With Hints on Pronunciation

“Regular” Verbs

[<u>–d</u> & <u>–ed</u> endings]

agreed
asked **[t]**
called
continued
covered
decided
designed
died
failed
finished **[t]** *[try long **<u>sh-</u>**]*
floated
followed
learned
lived
made
needed
noted
offered

[Unusual: Final –t sounds for –ed]

Col. A, 2
Col. B, 3

% of Final –t sound 5/39 = 12.8%

Past Tense Verbs - VOA

played
powered
printed
produced **[t]**
proved
returned
said
seemed
sold
solved
started
stayed
stopped **[t]**
tested
traveled
tried
turned
used
watched **[t]** [**x** Watch it!]
weighed
worked

Regular Verb Count [–d or –ed endings]

Col. A, 18
<u>Col. B, 21</u>

Subtotal 39

Total Verbs Listed = 53

% regular verbs = 39/53

≈ 74%, about 3 out of 4.

“Irregular” Verbs

[internal changes—

or none!]

began
broke
brought
built
flew
gave
read * *[Sounds like **<u>red</u>**]*
rose
taught
thought
took
tore
wrote
written

Irregular Verb Count
Col. C = Subtotal 14

* read, read, read
is irregular in its own way!
<u>Sound</u> changes, but all 3
<u>spellings</u> are the same.

% irregular = 14/53 ≈ 26%, or about 1 in 4.

(Rev. 6), 2009.8.26
Notes by mns

The Wright Brothers: They Showed the World How to Fly

In 1903, they made the world's first flight in a machine that was heavier than air and powered by an engine.
Transcript of radio broadcast:
15 September 2007

MP3 - Download Audio
Listen to MP3

ANNOUNCER:

Welcome to People in America from VOA Special English. Today, Sarah Long and Rich Kleinfeldt tell the story of Wilbur and Orville Wright. The Wright brothers made a small engine-powered flying machine and proved that it was possible for humans to really fly.

(MUSIC)

VOICE ONE:

Wilbur Wright was born in eighteen sixty-seven near Melville, Indiana. His brother Orville was born four years later in Dayton, Ohio.

Wilbur Wright

Throughout their lives, they were best friends. As Wilbur once said: "From the time we were little children, Orville and I lived together, played together, worked together and thought together."

Wilbur and Orville's father was a bishop, an official of the United Brethren Church. He traveled a lot on church business. Their mother was unusual for a woman of the nineteenth century. She had completed college. She was especially good at mathematics and science. And she was good at using tools to fix things or make things.

VOICE TWO:

Orville Wright

One winter day when the Wright brothers were young, all their friends were outside sliding down a hill on wooden sleds. The Wright brothers were sad, because they did not have a sled. So, Missus Wright said she would make one for them. She drew a picture of a sled. It did not look like other sleds. It was lower to the ground and not as wide. She told the boys it would be faster, because there would be less resistance from the wind when they rode on it. Missus Wright was correct. When the sled was finished, it was the fastest one around. Wilbur and Orville felt like they were flying.

The sled project taught the Wright brothers two

important rules. They learned they could increase speed by reducing wind resistance. And they learned the importance of drawing a design. Missus Wright said: "If you draw it correctly on paper, it will be right when you build it."

VOICE ONE:

When Wilbur was eleven years old and Orville seven, Bishop Wright brought home a gift for them. It was a small flying machine that flew like helicopters of today. It was made of paper, bamboo and cork.

The motor was a rubber band that had to be turned many times until it was tight. When the person holding the toy helicopter let go, it rose straight up. It stayed in the air for a few seconds. Then it floated down to the floor.

Wilbur and Orville played and played with their new toy. Finally, the paper tore and the rubber band broke. They made another one. But it was too heavy to fly. Their first flying machine failed.

VOICE TWO:

Their attempts to make the toy gave them a new idea. They would make kites to fly and sell to their friends. They made many designs and tested them. Finally, they had the right design. The kites flew as though they had wings.

The Wright brothers continued to experiment with mechanical things. Orville started a printing business when he was in high school. He used a small printing machine to publish a newspaper. He sold copies of the newspaper to the other children in school, but he did not earn much money from the project.

VOICE ONE:

Wilbur offered some advice to his younger brother. Make the printing press bigger and publish a bigger newspaper, he said. So, together, they designed and built one. The machine looked strange. Yet it worked perfectly. Soon, Orville and Wilbur were publishing a weekly newspaper.

They also printed materials for local businessmen. They were finally earning money. Wilbur was twenty-five years old and Orville twenty-one when they began to sell and repair bicycles. Then they began to make them. But the Wright brothers never stopped thinking about flying machines.

VOICE TWO:

In eighteen ninety-nine, Wilbur decided to learn about all the different kinds of flying machines that had been designed and tested through the years. Wilbur wrote to the Smithsonian Institution in Washington. He asked for all the information it had on flying.

The Wright brothers read everything they could about people who sailed through the air under huge balloons. They also read about people who tried to fly on gliders—planes with wings, but no motors.

VOICE ONE:

Then the Wright brothers began to design their own flying machine. They used the ideas they had developed from their earlier experiments with the toy helicopter, kites, printing machine and bicycles.

Soon, they needed a place to test their ideas about flight. They wrote to the Weather Bureau in Washington to find the place with the best wind conditions. The best place seemed to be a thin piece of sandy land in North Carolina along the coast of the Atlantic Ocean. It was called Kill Devil Hill, near the town of Kitty Hawk. It had the right wind and open space. Best of all, it was private.

VOICE TWO:

In nineteen hundred, the Wright brothers tested a glider that could carry a person.

But neither the first or second glider they built had the lifting power needed for real flight. Wilbur and Orville decided that what they had read about air pressure on curved surfaces was wrong. So they built a wind tunnel two meters long in their bicycle store in Dayton, Ohio. They tested more than two hundred designs of wings. These tests gave them the correct information about air pressure on curved surfaces. Now it was possible for them to design a machine that could fly.

A Wright glider from 1901

VOICE ONE:

The Wright brothers built a third glider. They took it to Kitty Hawk in the summer of nineteen-oh-two. They made almost one thousand flights with the glider. Some covered more than one hundred eighty meters. This glider proved that they had solved most of the problems of balance in flight. By the autumn of nineteen-oh-three, Wilbur and Orville had designed and built an airplane powered by a gasoline engine. The plane had wings twelve meters across. It weighed about three hundred forty kilograms, including the pilot.

VOICE TWO:

The Wright Brothers' first flight

The Wright brothers returned to Kitty Hawk. On December seventeen, nineteen-oh-three, they made the world's first flight in a machine that was heavier than air and powered by an engine. Orville flew the plane thirty-seven meters. He was in the air for twelve seconds. The two brothers made three more flights that day. The longest was made by Wilbur. He flew two hundred sixty meters in fifty-nine seconds.

Four other men watched the Wright brothers' first flights. One of the men took pictures. Few newspapers, however, noted the event.

VOICE ONE:

Wilbur and Orville returned home to Ohio. They built more powerful engines and flew better airplanes. But their success was almost unknown. Most people still did not believe flying was possible. It was almost five years before the Wright brothers became famous. In nineteen-oh-eight, Wilbur went to France. He gave demonstration flights at heights of ninety meters. A French company agreed to begin making the Wright brothers' flying machine.

VOICE TWO:

Orville made successful flights in the United States at the time Wilbur was in France. One lasted an hour. Orville also made fifty-seven complete circles over a field at Fort Myer, Virginia. The United States War Department agreed to buy a Wright brothers' plane. Wilbur and Orville suddenly became world heroes. Newspapers wrote long stories about them. Crowds followed them. But they were not seeking fame. They returned to Dayton where they continued to improve their airplanes. They taught many others how to fly.

VOICE ONE:

Wilbur Wright died of typhoid fever in nineteen twelve. Orville Wright continued designing and inventing until he died many years later, in nineteen forty-eight.

Today, the Wright brothers' first airplane is in the Air and Space Museum in Washington, D.C. Visitors to the museum look at the Wright brothers' small plane with its cloth wings, wooden controls and tiny engine. Then they see space vehicles and a rock collected from the moon. This is striking evidence of the changes in the world since Wilbur and Orville Wright began the modern age of flight, one hundred years ago.

(MUSIC)

ANNOUNCER:

This program was written by Marilyn Rice Christiano and produced by Paul Thompson. Your announcers were Sarah Long and Rich Kleinfeldt. I'm Faith Lapidus. Join us again next week for People in America from VOA Special English.

Instructor's Notes: *This typeface (font) is Verdana 10.5.*

Readability Statistics: *[from Tools Menu, Spelling & Grammar Check]*

Counts: *Words 1443, Characters 7027, Paragraphs 52 [?!], Sentences 126*

Averages: *Sentences/Paragraph 4.7, Words/Sentence 10.9, Characters/Word 4.7*

Readability: *Passives 3%, Flesch Reading Ease 74.1, Grade Level 5.6*

Powered Flight—in English!

Complete these basic math questions. Then let's discuss your reasoning in class.

Major ____________ Student # ______________ Name ______________ Date ____________

Major ____________ Student # ______________ Name ______________ Date ____________

On Dec. 17, 1903, the Wright brothers "made the world's first flight in a machine that was heavier than air and powered by an engine. Orville flew the plane thirty-seven meters. He was in the air for twelve seconds.

"The two brothers made three more flights that day. The longest was made by Wilbur. He flew two hundred sixty meters in fifty-nine seconds." *[Quotation from VOA Broadcast & Script]*

<u>Questions: Simple calculations using time and distance</u>

1) Calculate the flying speed (velocity) for the <u>first</u> successful flight.

Answer 1) The flying speed for the first flight was __________ meters per second.

2) Calculate the flying speed (velocity) for the <u>longest</u> flight that day.

Answer 2) The flying speed for the longest flight that day was _____________ m/s.

3) What was the <u>increase</u> in speed for the longest flight compared to the first? Write your answer as a percentage.

Answer 3) The speed (velocity) of the longest flight was _______ % greater (more).

4) Compare the <u>duration</u> (length of time) of these two flights. How much longer was the longest flight than the first one? (A simple, whole-number answer is fine.)

Answer 4) The longest flight lasted ____ seconds; the first flight was in the air ____ seconds. So, the longest flight was about _____ times as long as the first one.

5) In 1908, Orville made one flight that lasted an hour. Compare this new time to the longest flight time on day one (1903). Answer in percent.

Answer 5) The flight time increased from about ____ minute on day one (Dec. 17, 1903) to ____ minutes in 1908. So, in five years, the Wright brothers were able to increase their flying time by _____________________ percent.

Statistics (V-8): Words 295; s/p 2.0, w/s 10.5, passives 3%; Reading Ease 79.2, Grade Level 4.7

Powered flight, Qns *Technical Writing, An Introduction* *2009.5 © Michael Neil Shapiro*

PART 10 - MANUALS

Instruction Manuals / Owner's Manuals / Users Manuals

A Brief Review Before We Get Into Manuals

Introduction to Manuals (Lecture Content)

Electric Kettle Booklet

What Is CE Marking?

► Questions on Electric Kettle Booklet

Electric Shaver Manual

► Questions on Electric Shaver Manual

Memo - Pilot Light

Teaching Points:

Features; Fonts; Organizing Methods; CE Marking

★ Graded Assignment – Instruction Manuals 20% ★

A Brief Review Before We Get Into Manuals

(Notes for the Board, After the Mid-Term Exam Break)

Technically Correct Sentences

Begin with a Capital letter (대문자).
End with a "stop" sign (. ? !).
Put a verb into the sentence. An ACTIVE verb is usually best.

Paragraphing

Use one of three (3) standard paragraph styles: indented, block, or combination.

Technical Tools to Help Us

Use Spell check and Grammar check in MS-Word proofing tools.
Turn on and use Readability scores / statistics to improve your work.

Written Assignments We Did

Completed the Resumé form.
Wrote a Job Application (Cover) Letter using the Technical Tools in MS-Word.

VOA

We listened to two VOA programs and read their scripts. We noticed how VOA writers prepared the Special English scripts to help their listeners understand, by using:

- Short sentences and active verbs.
- Simple vocabulary (1500 words).

We practiced "listen and say" for the past tense verbs in "The Wright Brothers". You answered questions in writing on both these VOA radio scripts.

*   *   *

Statistics: Words 158; s/p 1.1, w/s 8.4; p/s (passive sentences) 0%, Reading ease 72.8, Grade level 5.1

◊

An observation: *What's amazing to me each semester is how diligent, suddenly, my much-chastened, post-mid-term students have become, as they copy these notes from the Board. But it's all to the good.*

Brief Review (V-3) *Technical Writing, An Introduction* *2009.10.28 © mns*

INTRODUCTION TO MANUALS

(Lecture Content)

MANU – is a Latin root-word, meaning **HAND.**

So a MANUAL is a HANDBOOK.

This means that the book is small enough to carry in your hand, or it's useful enough that you should keep it near your hand. It's a "handy" reference book, even if it's a huge and heavy auto-parts manual that sits on its own table.

In the past, people used to make things they needed by hand. When we make things by hand, we **manufacture** them. *MANU-* [hand] + *FACERE* [make]

For mass production, a lot of workers make a lot of things, together. And they use machines. So, they can't work at home. They need a special, building. In the past, people called that place a MANU-FACTORY. But "manufactory" is pretty long to say. So now we just say FACTORY.

Most products we buy, especially electrical or electronic products, come with **written instructions on how to use and how to take care of the product.** This information can be on a single information sheet, on the folded pages of a pamphlet, or in a little book, or booklet.

People call this written document an **Owner's Manual, a User's Manual or an Instruction Manual.** They all mean about the same. And somebody—or a team—has to write this manual. You might be a member of that team.

So let's learn what goes into a manual, and what features make it a good one. **A handbook that helps us use a product correctly is a good example of "technical writing" that's useful in our daily life.**

We'll examine the **form** and the **content** of two manuals. Then you'll answer a few questions about each one. I will give you time in class to write your answers. By doing this work, you'll develop your ideas about what is good and not so good in each manual.

When the time comes, I hope you will apply what you learned.

Statistics (V-10): Words 324; s/p 2.6, w/s 12.1; passives 0%, Reading ease 78.2, Grade level 5.3

Manuals, Intro Lecture *Technical Writing, An Introduction* *2009.11.02 © mns*

PL

Czajnik elektryczny

SWK 1500

Czyszczenie filtra i czajnika

Dający się wyjąć filtr służy do zatrzymywania osadów gromadzących się na grzałce i zapobiega ich wydostaniu się z czajnika w trakcie nalewania wody. Filtr ten należy regularnie czyścić przynajmniej pukając go pod bieżącą wodą.

Osady należy usuwać regularnie przynajmniej 1x w miesiącu.

Do usunięcia osadów z grzałki można użyć:

- 8% białego octu dostępnego we wszystkich sklepach. Do czajnika należy nalać do 1/2 l i pozostawić w czajniku bez gotowania przez 2 godziny. Potem należy ocet wylać i przegotować w nim 4–5 razy czystą wodę a następnie czajnik można ponownie używać do przygotowywania ciepłych napojów.
- kwaskiem cytrynowym. Zagotować 1/2 l wody i dodać do niej 30 g kwasku cytrynowego i pozostawić go w czajniku przez 30-ci minut. Potem należy wodę z kwaskiem wylać i przegotować w czajniku 4–5 razy czystą wodę. Potem czajnika można ponownie używać do przygotowywania ciepłych napojów.

Do czyszczenia zewnętrznych części czajnika należy używać suchej ściereczki lub wilgotnej ściereczki nasączonej płynem do mycia. Do czyszczenia podstawy należy używać jedynie suchej ściereczki. Do czyszczenia urządzenia nie należy używać rozpuszczalników lub rozcieńczalników, ew. środków czyszczących, które mogą porysować czyszczone powierzchnie i uszkodzić plastikowe elementy.

Dane techniczne:

230V ~ 50Hz, 2000 W
Objętość 1,5 l

Utylizacja niepotrzebnego sprzętu elektrycznego i elektronicznego

Taki symbol na produkcie lub na jego opakowaniu oznacza, że produkt nie może być traktowany jako odpad komunalny, lecz powinien być dostarczony do odpowiedniego punktu zbiórki sprzętu elektrycznego i elektronicznego, w celu przerobu i odzysku odpadów. W krajach Unii Europejskiej i w pozostałych krajach europejskich są odrębne systemy segregacji odpadów przeznaczone do utylizacji sprzętu elektrycznego i elektronicznego. Przez takie pro ekologiczne zachowanie zapobiegają Państwo potencjalnym negatywnym wpływom na środowisko naturalne oraz na zdrowie ludzi, jakie mogłyby wystąpić w przypadku niewłaściwego procesu składowania tego produktu. Przez zagospodarowanie materiałów oszczędzamy również surowce naturalne. Aby uzyskać bardziej szczegółowe informacje na temat przerobu i odzysku materiałów elektronicznych z tego produktu, proszę skontaktować się z urzędem miasta lub gminy, lokalnym zakładem utylizacji sprzętu elektrycznego i elektronicznego lub ze sklepem, w którym produkt został zakupiony.

Wskazówki i informacje dotyczące gospodarki z zużytymi opakowaniami

Zużyte opakowania należy składować w miejscu wyznaczonym przez władze lokalne, stosownym do przechowywania odpadu.

CE Produkt spełnia wszelkie wymogi i przepisy przewidziane dla tego typu produktu.

Electric Kettle

Instruction manual

EN

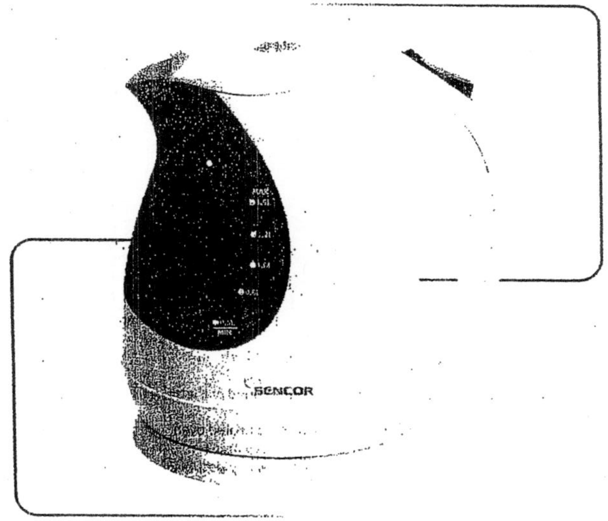

SENCOR®

SWK 1500

Warning

Extreme precaution should be exercised when using any type of domestic appliances, especially the followings:

- Before you plug the electric kettle in, check if the voltage specified on the label of the electric kettle corresponds to the mains voltage in your home.
- The base can be connected to the earthed wall socket only.
- Do not use the kettle in the immediate surroundings of a bath, a shower or a swimming pool.
- Only use the kettle in combination with original accessories.
- Do not place the kettle on windowsills. Always place the kettle on flat, dry surface.
- Make sure that the electrical cable and plug cannot come in contact with water or humidity.
- Do not spray the kettle with any liquid. Never immerse any part of the kettle in water or any other liquid.
- This kettle is for domestic use only and should not be used industrially. Do not use the kettle outdoors.
- Exercise extreme care whenever the kettle is to be used near the children.
- Disconnect the kettle from the power supply if it is to be moved, cleaned or if it is not used.
- Do not place the kettle on or near a hot gas or electric burner, or in a heated oven.
- Do not use the kettle if the electrical cable is damaged or whenever any possible internal failure or incorrect operation has been detected.
- Do not attempt to make any repairs yourself. Always contact the official repair services for either mechanical or electrical repairs.
- Do not let cord hang over edge of table or counter, or touch hot surfaces.
- Unplug the kettle by holding the plug; do not pull on the electrical cable.
- Do not use the kettle for other than intended use.
- Only use the kettle in combination with its original base.
- Before the kettle is used for making hot drinks, fill the kettle with clean water, boil the water and empty the kettle. The kettle is ready for common use after repeating this procedure for 5-6 times.
- This kettle should be used for boiling water only. Do not touch the lid while the kettle is boiling.
- Be careful, the body of metal kettle becomes hot while the water is boiling!

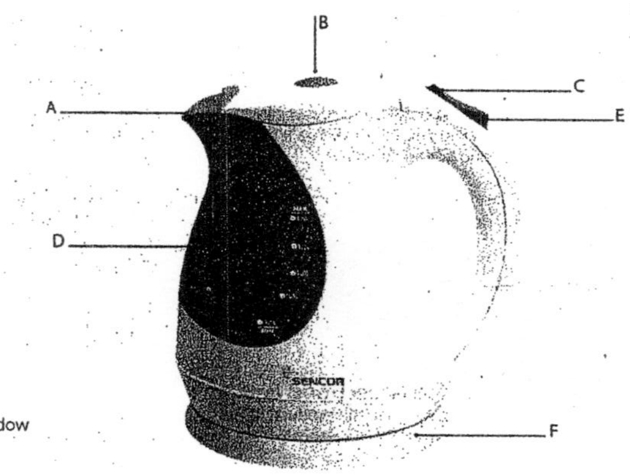

Description

A – Scale filter inside
B – Locking lid
C – Switch on/off
D – Water-level indication window
E – Indication light
F – 360° Rotational base

Instructions for use

- Remove all packaging from the kettle. Set the required length of the electrical cable.
- Place the base on flat, clean surface.
- Fill the kettle with required volume of clean water. Warning! If the kettle has been overfilled, there is a risk that boiling water will be ejected from the spout.
- Put the kettle on the base.
- Connect the plug to the wall socket.
- Push the switch button to the position „I".
- The kettle switches off automatically when the water has reached boiling point.
- Before removing the kettle from the base, make sure that the kettle switched off automatically, or switch it off by hand. The position „0" means the kettle is switched off, the position „I" means the kettle is switched on.
- Remove the plug from the wall socket and let the kettle cool down.
- The heating element of this kettle is protected by a safety cut-out device. This device will automatically switch the kettle off if it is accidentally switched on without any water or with insufficient water. Once the heating element is cooled down the kettle can be used again.
- You can fill the kettle with water either through the spout or through the open lid.
- Never fill the kettle below the minimum level.
- Do not fill the kettle when it is placed on the base.
- Never fill the kettle beyond the maximum level indication.
- Do not switch on the kettle without water.
- Make sure that the lid is properly closed before you switch the kettle on.

Electric Kettle

SWK 1500

Cleaning and descaling the kettle

In case of normal use, the following descaling frequency is recommended: once a month.

- 8% white vinegar. Fill the kettle with 1/2 l of 8% white vinegar and let it stand for two hours. Empty the kettle, fill it with clean water, boil the water and empty the kettle. It is recommended to boil pure water in the kettle 4-5 times before the kettle is used for preparing hot drinks again.

- citric acid. Boil 1/2 l water in the kettle, add 30 g of citric acid and let it stand for a half an hour. Empty the kettle, fill it with clean water, boil the water and empty the kettle. It is recommended to boil pure water in the kettle 4-5 times before the kettle is used for preparing hot drinks again.

Clean the outside of the kettle with a soft, damp cloth moistened with warm water and some mild cleaning agent. For cleaning the base use a dry cloth only. Do not use any abrasive cleaning agents, solvents etc. to clean the kettle.

Technical features

230V~50Hz, 2000 W
capacity 1,5 l

Disposal of Used Electrical & Electronic Equipment

The meaning of the symbol on the product, its accessory or packaging indicates that this product shall not be treated as household waste. Please, dispose of this equipment at your applicable collection point for the recycling of electrical & electronic equipments waste. In the European Union and Other European countries which there are separate collection systems for used electrical and electronic product. By ensuring the correct disposal of this product, you will help prevent potentially hazardous to the environment and to human health, which could otherwise be caused by unsuitable waste handling of this product. The recycling of materials will help conserve natural resources. Please do not therefore dispose of your old electrical and electronic equipment with your household waste. For more detailed information about recycling of this product, please contact your local city office, your household waste disposal service or the shop where you purchased the product.

Handling instructions for the disposal of used packaging material

Dispose of used packaging material properly. Use appropriate waste collection centres available at your location.

CE This product complies with all essential rules applicable to it.

Elektrická varná konvice

Návod k obsluze

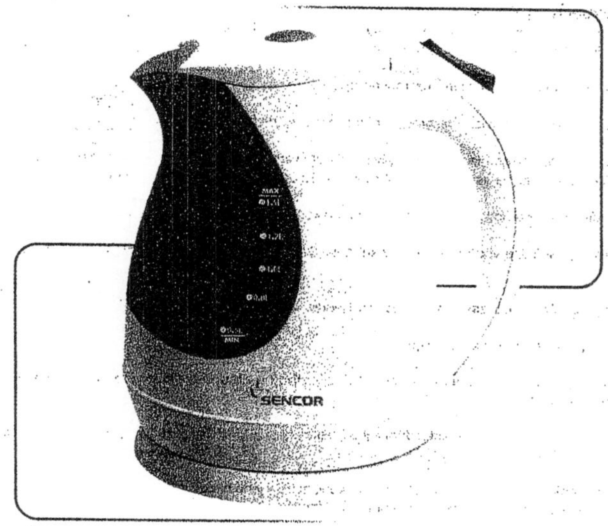

SENCOR®
SWK 1500

Před zapnutím přístroje se prosím seznamte s návodem k jeho obsluze, a to i v případě, že jste již obeznámeni s používáním přístrojů podobného typu. Používejte přístroj pouze tak, jak je popsáno v tomto návodu k použití. Návod uschovejte pro případ další potřeby.

Minimálně po dobu záruky doporučujeme uschovat originální přepravní karton, balicí materiál, pokladní doklad a záruční list. V případě přepravy zabalte přístroj opět do originální krabice od výrobce.

What
is CE Marking (CE Mark)?

What is CE Marking (CE Mark)?

CE Marking is the symbol CE as shown on the top of this page. The letters "**CE**" are the abbreviation of French phrase "**C**onformité **E**uropéen[n]e" which literally means "European Conformity". The term initially used was "EC Mark" and it was officially replaced by "CE Marking" in the Directive 93/68/EEC in 1993. "CE Marking" is now used in all EU official documents. "CE Mark" is also in use, but it is NOT the official term.

1. CE Marking on a product is a manufacturer's declaration that the product complies with the **essential requirements** of the relevant European health, safety and environmental protection legislation, in practice by many of the so-called Product Directives.*

   ***Product Directives** contain[s] the "essential requirements" and/or "performance levels" and "Harmonized Standards" to which the products must conform. Harmonized Standards are the technical specifications (European Standards or Harmonization Documents) which are established by several European standards agencies (CEN, CENELEC, etc).

   CEN stands for European Committee for Standardization.
   CENELEC stands for European Committee for Electrotechnical Standardization.

2. CE Marking on a product indicates to governmental officials that the product may be **legally placed on the market** in their country.
3. CE Marking on a product ensures the **free movement of the product** within the EFTA & European Union (EU) single market (total 28 countries), and
4. CE Marking on a product permits the **withdrawal of the non-conforming products** by customs and enforcement/vigilance authorities.

Along with more directives' becoming effective, more and more products are required to bear the CE Marking for gaining access to the EFTA & European Union market. However, <u>many non-EU exporters are still unaware of or unsure about this fact and its impact on their business.</u>

Please click the following links to learn more about every CE-Marking-related European Union Directive, Guidelines to Directives, Frameworks of implementation of Directives, and Agreements on Mutual Recognition of conformity assessment between European Union and other countries such as USA, Japan, Canada, Australia, New Zealand and Israel:-

1. Does my product need **CE Marking** in order to be sold/exported on/to the European Market?
2. How to obtain CE Marking for my product?
3. How can Wellkang Consultant Firm help me to obtain CE Marking for my product?
4. Wellkang can be your **Authorized Representative** in Europe for CE Marking purpose !
5. Buy a Directive or Guideline on Directive in Chinese, English, French, Portuguese and/or Spanish.
6. Complete list of all CE Marking Directives and Guidelines to Directives.

Statistics: Words 414; s/p 1.9, w/s 15.8; passives 19%, Reading Ease 42.1, grade level 11.3

http://www.ce-marking.com/what-is-CE-marking.html

ELECTRIC KETTLE BOOKLET: QUESTIONS

SENCOR SWK1500

1. What kind of booklet is this? *[See page 1, subtitle on black Title bar.]*

   Answer: It's ________________________________. (1)

2. What or whom is the manufacturer trying to protect by printing all the warnings in the manual? ○ ____________ ○ ____________ ○ ____________ (3)

3. Before using the kettle to make hot drinks, what should the owner do? *[See p. 2]*

   Note: Write four (4) complete, short, sentences. Begin each sentence with an active verb.

   Answers: i) ________________________________

   ii) ________________________________

   iii) ________________________________

   iv) ________________________________. (2)

4. Name ONE big problem you have found in using this manual. (1)

   Answer: ____

5. "Do not attempt to make any repairs yourself. Always contact the official repair services for either mechanical or electrical repairs." On what page can I find out how to contact the official repair services? ________________________ (1)

6. In CE Marking, what do the letters CE mean?

   Answer: They mean __________________ __________________. (1)

7. Why is this CE symbol printed on this manual and on the electric kettle? (1)

   Answer: It's printed on the kettle and on the manual to show that this product

   ____.

Total _____/10

Statistics: words 169; s/p 5.0, w/s 8.7; Readability: passives 6%, Reading ease 76.5, Grade Level 4.7

Manual EK (V-24) *Technical Writing, An Introduction* *mns © 2009.11.5*

HQ663, HQ662

Important

- Only use the HQ600 powerplug supplied to charge the shaver.
- The powerplug transforms 100-240 Volts to 12 Volts.
- Make sure the HQ600 powerplug does not get wet.
- The shaver runs at a safe low voltage of 12 Volts. It is watertight and can be cleaned under the tap. Do not rinse it with water hotter than 80°C.

Charge indications

- As soon as you start charging the shaver, the green pilot light will go on.
- When the battery has been fully charged, the green pilot light will start blinking.

Charging

Recharge the shaver at a temperature between 5°C and 35°C.
The powerplug is suitable for mains voltages ranging from 100 to 240V.

- The shaver does not work while charging. This means that you won' t be able to use the appliance when it is recharging.

To extend the lifetime of the battery, do not leave the shaver connected to the mains continuously.

1 Put the appliance plug in the shaver.

2 Put the powerplug in the wall socket.
Do not recharge the shaver in a closed pouch.

3 When charging for the first time or after a long period of disuse: leave the shaver to charge continuously for 12 hours.
Charging normally takes approx. 8 hours.

4 To extend the lifetime of the battery, remove the powerplug from the wall socket and pull the appliance plug out of the shaver when the battery has been fully charged.

A fully charged shaver has a cordless shaving time of up to approx. 30 minutes.

Shaving

1 Remove the appliance plug from the shaver before you start shaving.

2 Switch the shaver on by pressing the on/off button once.

3 Move the shaving heads over the skin, making both straight and circular movements.
Shaving on a dry face gives the best results.
Your skin may need 2-3 weeks to get accustomed to the Philishave system.

4 Switch the shaver off by pressing the on/off button again.

Replace the shaving heads (type HQ6 Quadra Action) every 2 years for optimal shaving results.

Trimming

For grooming sideburns and moustache.

1 Open the trimmer by pushing the slide upwards.

The trimmer can be activated while the motor is running.

Cleaning

Regular cleaning guarantees better shaving results.

Shaving unit

When you clean the appliance, it is not necessary to take the shaving heads (cutters and guards) apart. If you want to take them apart, be sure not to mix up the cutters and guards, since grinding of the cutters in the guards only guarantees optimal performance for each matching set. If you accidentally mix up the sets, it could take several weeks before optimal shaving performance is restored.

The easiest and most hygienic way to clean the shaver is to rinse the shaving unit with hot water once a week (60°C-80°C).

1 Switch the shaver off, remove the powerplug from the wall socket and pull the appliance plug out of the shaver.

2 Press the release button to open the shaving unit.

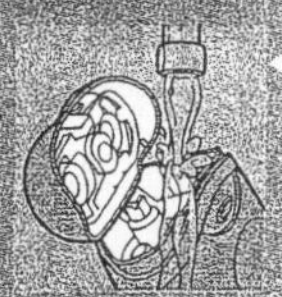

3 Clean the shaving unit and the hair chamber by rinsing them under a hot tap (60°C-80°C) for some time.

4 Close the shaving unit and shake off the water.

Do not dry the shaving unit with a towel or a tissue; this could cause damage to the shaving heads.

1 Open the shaving unit again to let both the shaving unit and the hair chamber dry properly.

- You can also clean the hair chamber without water by using the brush supplied.

Trimmer

Clean the trimmer every time you have used it.

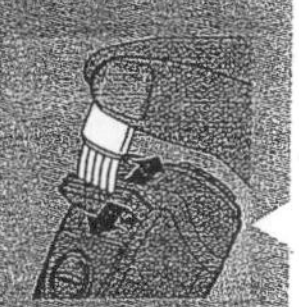

1 Switch the shaver off, remove the powerplug from the wall socket and pull the appliance plug out of the shaver.

2 Clean the trimmer with the brush.

3 Lubricate the trimmer teeth with a drop of sewing machine oil every six months.

Replacing the shaving heads

Replace the shaving heads every two years for optimal shaving results.

1 Switch the shaver off, remove the powerplug from the socket and pull the appliance plug out of the shaver.

2 Press the release button to open the shaving unit.

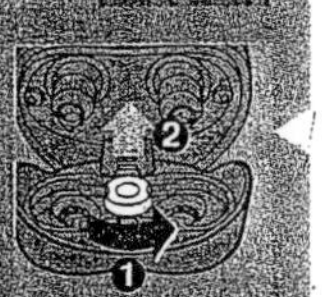

3 Turn the wheel anti-clockwise (1) and remove the retaining frame (2).

4 Remove the shaving heads and place the new ones in the shaving unit in such a way that the projections fit exactly into the recesses in the shaving unit.

5 Reassemble the shaving unit by pressing the wheel and turning it clockwise.

6 Close the shaving unit.

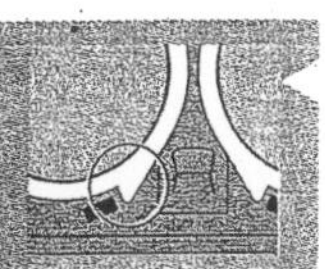

- If the shaving heads have been properly inserted, the shiny parts are pointing inwards and towards each other.

Replace damaged or worn shaving heads with Philishave HQ6 Quadra Action shaving heads only.

Storing

- Put the protection cap on the shaver to prevent damage.
- Store the shaver in the pouch.

Disposal of the battery

Remove the battery when you discard the shaver. Do not throw the battery away with the normal household waste, but hand it in at an official collection point. You can also take the battery to a Philips Service Centre in your country, which will dispose of it in an environmentally safe way.

Only remove the battery if it is completely empty.

1 Remove the powerplug from the wall socket and pull the appliance plug out of the shaver.

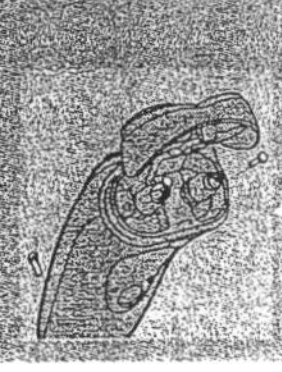

2 Let the shaver run until it stops, undo the screws and open the shaver.

3 Remove the battery.

The shaver should not be connected to the mains again after the battery has been removed.

Troubleshooting

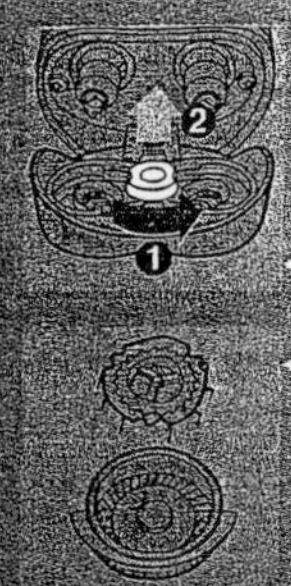

1 Reduced shaving performance

- *Cause 1: The shaving heads are dirty. The shaver has not been rinsed long enough or the water used was not hot enough.*

- **Clean the shaver thoroughly before you continue shaving (See 'Cleaning').**

- *Cause 2: Long hairs are obstructing the shaving heads.*

- **Remove the retaining frame.**
- **Remove the hairs.**
- **Clean the cutters and guards.**

Do not clean more than one cutter and guard at a time, since they are all matching sets. If you accidentally mix up the cutters and guards, it could take several weeks before optimal shaving performance is restored.

- **Put the retaining frame back onto the shaving unit.**

- *Cause 3: Shaving heads are damaged or worn.*

- **Remove the retaining frame.**

- **Remove the old shaving heads from the shaving unit and replace them with new ones.**

Damaged or worn shaving heads (cutters and guards) must only be replaced with original Philishave HQ6 Quadra Action shaving heads!

- **Put the retaining frame back onto the shaving unit.**

2 The shaver does not work when the on/o[ff] button is pressed:

- *Cause 1: The shaver is connected to the mains.*

- **Disconnect the shaver from the mains.**

- *Cause 2: The battery is empty.*

- **Recharge the battery.**

Guarantee & service

If you need service or information or if you have a problem, please visit the Philips Web site at www.philips.com or contact the Philips Customer Care Centre in your country (you will find its phone number in the worldwide guarantee leaflet). If there is no Customer Care Centre in your country, turn to your local Philips dealer or contact the Service Department of Philips Domestic Appliances and Personal Care BV.

ELECTRIC SHAVER BOOKLET: QUESTIONS

Philishave 600 Series by Philips

1. **How many pages** of instructions are in this booklet? Answer: __________ ( ) (1)

2. **Instructions are available** in ____________________ ( ) languages. (1)

3. **List, in order,** the eleven main section headings (in the black bars): ______________ (1)

________________________ ________________ ________________ ________________

________________ __________________________________ ________________

____________________________ ____________________ ________________________

4. **List three (3) features** that make this manual easy to read, understand and use.

-
-
- (1)

5. **Can I clean** this electric shaver using running water? YES / NO (Circle your answer.) (1)

6. How do I know when the battery is fully charged? (To answer, write a sentence.)

____.(1)

7. **Can I shave** with the power cord plugged in? YES / NO (Circle your answer.) (1)

8. **How long** will this electric razor (or shaver) work on battery power after it's fully charged?*

Answer BRIEFLY: ____(1)

9. **Thinking Qn:** List two factors that can affect how long the razor works on one charge. (2)

▶

▶

Total _____/10

* **Discuss the difference** between "approximately" (about) *[= + / -]* and "up to" *[= max. or limit].*

Stats (V-23): words 159; s/p 3.0, w/s 10.2; Readability: passives 0%, Reading ease 67.8, Grade Level 6.3

Manuals Exercise Technical Writing, An Introduction 2009.11 (2008) © mns

MEMO ON ELECTRIC SHAVER MANUAL

Philishave 600 Series by Philips

"Lead, Kindly Light, amidst th' encircling gloom."

(Hymn, words written in 1833 by John Henry Newman)

PILOT LIGHT

A pilot light is single gas flame, for example on a boiler. The pilot light is always on. When more hot water is needed, the pilot light ignites the main burner. Then, the boiler can produce more hot water for washing dishes or clothes, or for taking a shower.

"Pilot light" here is an error in fact. The manual writer should have said, "indicator light" or "LED light". LED means Light Emitting Diode. So, saying LED, by itself, is enough. However, it's often wise to add a familiar word (light) to explain a less familiar term, such as LED. The charge indicator on this electric shaver is, in fact, an LED.

Most electronic equipment today uses one or more LED's to show that it's functioning.

As we will read in the essay, "How to read a scientific paper critically,"

"NOT EVERYTHING YOU SEE IN PRINT IS NECESSARILY CORRECT OR TRUE."

And here we have proof of that!

MNS

2009.12

Stats (V-8): words 188; s/p 2.3, w/s 10.7; Readability: passives 7%, Reading ease 72.6, Grade Level 5.8

PART 11 - RULES OF THUMB

"Rule of Thumb" (R.O.T.), Some Definitions

Some Rules Of Thumb, Cited

► Picture This! Draw & label a simple diagram to show Rule of Thumb info.

Teaching Points:

Work with brief "technical" descriptions, written in English.

Rules of Thumb

Some Definitions

Rule of thumb *n.* **1.** a general principle or rule based on experience or practice, as opposed to a scientific calculation. **2.** a rough, practical method of procedure [1685-95]

Statistics: Words 29, Reading Ease 59.2, Grade Level 7.6

Random House Webster's College Dictionary, page 1153b
Second Revised and Updated Random House Edition, April 2000.

One Instructor's versions (short & long):

A rule of thumb is a rough guide to action.

Statistics: Words 10, Reading Ease 100.0, Grade Level 1.2

OR

A rule of thumb is a statement of practical information based on experience.

Statistics: Words 13, Reading Ease 50.4, Grade Level 9.4

What's YOUR version?

____

____

Statistics: Words ___, Reading Ease ___, Grade Level ___

RULES OF THUMB

The following items are excerpts from *Rules of Thumb,* a book by Tom Parker.
He says, **"It is not a book of facts; it is a book of experience."***

USING A MOVIE CAMERA Count at least ten seconds every time you press a movie camera's start button. The biggest single error that novice filmmakers make is taking many shots in very short spurts. *Flip Schulke, underwater photographer*

DEALING WITH DOUBT (EDITING) When in doubt, cross it out.
Bryant Robey, editor, American Demographics magazine

SHOOTING AT HELICOPTERS North Vietnamese ground troops used their thumbs to determine whether they could reach enemy aircraft with hand-held weapons. If an airplane or helicopter was bigger than a thumb held at arm's length, they could bring it down with ground fire. *D. Tanner, Fort Wayne, Indiana*

SAVING MONEY You should have six months' salary in savings for emergencies.
Bob Horton, statistics consultant, West Lafayette, Indiana

READING A MAP You can tell where a map of the world was made by seeing which country is smack dab in the middle. *Adham Loutfi, Oakland, California*

AIMING A SOLAR WATER HEATER For year-round use, the slope of home hot water solar collectors should be equal to the latitude at which they are installed.
Stephen Gibian, architect and stonemason, Ithaca, New York

BUYING A CAR When you buy a used car, replace all of its fluids, even the brake fluid. The water that accumulates in old fluid will slowly rust the parts that it touches.
Al Kaehler, mechanical engineer, Mountain View, California

CHECKING AN EGG When placed in a bowl of water, a fresh egg will sink and lie on its side. An egg that's not fresh but still edible will sink and stand partially erect on its tapered end. A rotten egg will float. *David Hechler, writer, Rockport, Texas*

PROOFREADING If you find one error while proofreading, there are likely to be several more in the same or contiguous paragraphs. *Cheryl Russell, demographer*

JOB INTERVIEWING During a job interview, never spend more than sixty seconds answering a question. *Cheryl Russell, demographer*

WRITING AN ADVERTISEMENT When writing an ad, use sentences of less than twelve words. *David Ogilvy, advertising expert, The Ogilvy and Mather Agency*

DOUBLING YOUR MONEY You can quickly calculate the number of years it will take to double your money by dividing the number seventy-two by your interest rate. If your money is invested at 6-percent interest, it will take 72 / 6 = 12 years to double.

Steve Parker, aerospace engineer, Princeton, New Jersey

MAKING A DECISION There are three valid answers to a yes or no question: yes, no, and no decision right now. Eighty percent of all bad decisions are snap decisions. Good managers make the best decisions after "sleeping on it".

Joseph Stein, business consultant, Arcata, California

EATING MEALS Most people eat their largest meal at supper, when their bodies need it least. As a rule, you should eat breakfast like a king, lunch like a prince, and supper like a pauper. *Jane Brody, nutrition columnist, The New York Times*

DESIGNING ADVERTISEMENTS Five times as many people read the headline as read the rest of an ad. *David Ogilvy, advertising expert, The Ogilvy and Mather Agency*

THE SURVIVAL RULE OF THREE You can live three seconds without blood, three minutes without air, three days without water, and three weeks without food.

Sandy Figuers, geologist, El Paso, Texas

TEACHING To teach effectively, a teacher should limit a class to twenty-five students. *Leslie Warren, music teacher, Kittery Point, Maine*

THE TRAVELING RULE OF TWO When traveling, take twice the money and half the clothes you think you will need. *Betsy Wackernagel, Ithaca, New York*

TRYING A NEW IDEA It takes three tries to get a new idea right, especially if a physical prototype is involved. The first try reveals any obvious short-comings, and the second try cleans these up so you can see what you really need to do.

J. Baldwin, designer and writer

CARRYING THINGS You can lift, for a short time, twice your weight. You can carry and move your own weight. For a long distance you can carry, uncomfortably, half your weight, or comfortably, one-fourth your weight. *J. Baldwin, designer and writer*

SETTING YOUR RATES Free-lance artists and graphic designers should determine their hourly rate [in dollars] by dividing [the annual income they need] by one thousand. *Mike Rider, art director*

THINGS THAT BITE As a matter of biology rather than sexism, if something bites you, it is probably female. *Scott M. Kruse, Yosemite National Park, California*

CHOOSING PAPER FOR BROCHURES Men respond best to smooth, coated paper; women respond best to textured, uncoated paper. *Anne Trovinger, graphic designer*

DRIVING ON ICE AND SNOW Second gear is the best one for driving on ice and snow. *Leslie Warren, music teacher, Kittery Point, Maine*

STARTING A BUSINESS VENTURE the idea for a new venture is likely to be strategically unsound if it can't be put into one coherent sentence. *Kenichi Ohmae, The Mind of the Strategist*

REPEATING AN EXPERIMENT If you can't repeat your own experiment, you're probably not doing science. If no one else can repeat your experiment, you are probably lying. *Gary Marlow, scientist, Ithaca, New York*

THE RULE OF 80-20 Eighty percent of the benefit comes from twenty percent of the effort. So, by choosing carefully, you can do 20% of the jobs in front of you and get 80% of the benefit. *Alan Lakein, author; Ray Bruman, Berkeley, California, and others*

TURNING OFF YOUR ENGINE It pays to turn off your engine if it will be idling for more than one minute. *Owen Chambers, petroleum distributor*

Statistics: words 940; s/p 4.0, w/s 17.5; passives 9%, Reading ease 86.1, Grade level 7.9

Parker, Tom. **Rules of Thumb, Houghton, Mifflin, Boston, 1983. Introduction.*

Rules of Thumb *Body Arial 11; Sources, Arial 10, Italic. Title, Arial 16* *Total 28 tems*

Picture This!

A Really Challenging Exercise in Technical Writing

(Converting Words to Pictures)

- **Make a simple diagram or sketch for two of these four Rules of Thumb*.**
- **Label each diagram to show all key facts and physical relationships.**
- **Then we'll have some volunteers put their drawings on the Board.**
- **People who draw the information correctly deserve a prize!**

CHECKING AN EGG When placed in a bowl of water, a fresh egg will sink and lie on its side. An egg that's not fresh but still edible will sink and stand partially erect on its tapered end. A rotten egg will float. *David Hechler, writer, Rockport, Texas*

AIMING A SOLAR WATER HEATER for year-round use, the slope of home hot water solar collectors should be equal to the latitude at which they are installed.

Stephen Gibian, architect and stonemason, Ithaca, New York

Tougher Challenges?

USING PULLEYS Two pulleys connected by a belt should be separated by at least the difference between their individual diameters.

John H. Parker, mechanical engineer

DESIGNING A SUBMARINE A submarine will move through the water most efficiently if it has a length-to-beam ratio of between 10 to 1 and 13 to 1.

Brent Wiggins, artist and military buff

Question: If this was the final exam, could you pass? It's Technical Writing in English.

Statistics (V-6): words 216; s/p 1.4, w/s 12.9; passives 14%, Reading ease 67.9, Grade level 6.9

Parker, Tom. **Rules of Thumb, Houghton, Mifflin, Boston, 1983. Introduction.*

PART 12 - TECHNICAL WRITING for PUBLICATION

Academic & Professional Publication

Code of Ethics (Excerpt)

National Society of Professional Engineers (NSPE) [U.S.A.]
Definition of Plagiarism
Difference Between Scholarship And Theft
- Simply Giving Credit Where It Is Due

Press / News Release

Hyundai Motor Manufacturing Czech (HMMC), Press Release
& Exercise (Create Your Own)

Advanced Academic Reading:

Advance Vocabulary for "How to read a scientific paper critically"
How to read a scientific paper- critically!
۞ 과학논문을 비판적으로 읽으려면
- Korean language version & critical commentary

Advanced Academic Writing

► Proofread & Re-write a Medical Research excerpt
Fair Use Guidelines: U.S. Copyright Office

Teaching Points:

Write shorter sentences. Use spell check.

Write active sentences as much as possible.

Use Readability statistics to improve your written work.

Read all professional writing critically!

CODE OF ETHICS
OF THE
NATIONAL SOCIETY OF PROFESSIONAL ENGINEERS (NSPE) [U.S.A.]
Part III, Professional Obligations

9. Engineers shall give credit for engineering work to those to whom credit is due, and will recognize the proprietary interests of others. *[Emphasis added.]*

a. Engineers shall, whenever possible, name the person or persons who may be individually responsible for designs, inventions, writings, or other accomplishments.

Statistics: Words 61, Sent. 2; w/s 22.5; passives 0%; Reading Ease 26.0, Grade Level 15.2

Reprinted by Permission of the National Society of Professional Engineers (NSPE), www.nspe.org

Also cited in Saeed Moaveni, ***Engineering Fundamentals, An Introduction to Engineering,*** Brooks/Cole, the Wadsworth Group, a division of Thompson Learning, Inc., 2002, page 398.

Definition of Plagiarism*

plagiarism (plā' jə riz' əm, -jē ə riz'-) *n.* **1.** the unauthorized use of the language and thoughts of another author and the representation of them as one's own. 2. something used and represented in this manner. [1615-25] **–plagiarist**, *n.* **–plagiaristic**, *adj.*

plagiarize (plā' jə rīz', -jē ə rīz'-) *v.* **–rized, -rizing.** *–v.t.* **1.** to take and use by plagiarism. **2.** to take and use ideas, passages, etc., from (another's work) by plagiarism. *–v.i.* **3.** to commit plagiarism.

**Random House Webster's College Dictionary*, page 1011a
Second Revised and Updated Random House Edition, April 2000.

So, the difference between scholarship and theft

is simply giving credit where it's due.

MNS

Statistics (V-10): words 227; s/p 2.5, w/s 9.3; passives 0%, reading ease 44.6, grade level 9.3

Thursday, 13. November 2008

TODAY HMMC DONATED 28 HYUNDAI i30 CARS TO THE TECHNICAL SCHOOLS

This afternoon Hyundai Motor Manufacturing Czech plant in Nošovice witnessed an extraordinary event. Representatives of nine secondary and vocational schools from Ostrava, Frydek-Mistek, Koprivnice, Bruntal and Zabreh na Morave and representatives of the VSB Technical University of Ostrava and Police Academy of Jihlava received a symbolic key from the HMMC president Kim Eok-Jo, presenting the key to 28 Hyundai i30 cars that will serve as education tool[s] for future car mechanics and engineers.

All donated cars were made in the pilot production and cannot be used on the public roads. They will be utilized exclusively as static tools in the classes of schools that teach pupils and students in the advanced automotive technologies.

"The present from Hyundai Motor Manufacturing Czech given to you today is a symbolic expression of our commitment to be a good neighbor, reliable partner and responsible corporate member of both the Moravian-Silesian Region and Czech Republic," said Kim Eok-Jo, HMMC President, adding: "I wish that the cars submitted to you today serve well for the purpose defined and I believe that the fact that your students will learn about Hyundai technology in practice may affect their later career decisions."

"We want to deepen the cooperation with secondary technical schools and technical universities in the region, because future perfectly skilled and trained team members are the guarantee of quality production and our company development," said Kim Keun-Sik, HMMC Vice-President.

Petr Vaněk
General Manager, Public Relations Department

Statistics: Words 255; s/p 7.0, w/s 33.5; passives 28%, FRE 17.2, GL 19.1

www.**hyundai-motor.cz/hyundai**/english.php?rubrika=media&rok=2008

Reprinted with the kind permission of HMMC.

Published Technical Writing

CREATE YOUR OWN EXERCISE, OR MAKE YOUR OWN NOTES

for

"TODAY HMMC DONATED 28 HYUNDAI i30 CARS..."

Vocabulary for How to Read a Scientific Paper Critically

(Listen and Say)

Verbs

abstract
addressed **[t]**
asserted
bogged down
cited
copied
edited[1]
entered
expanded
frustrated
interested[1]
interpreted
listed
mentioned
modified
passed **[t]**[2]
persuaded
prepared
presented
proven[1]
raised
reported
resolved
suggested
taken[1]
tested
trapped **[t]**
used

Nouns

Abstract
assumptions
faculties
hypotheses **[-eez]**[3]
hypothesis
interpretation
Introduction
purpose
References
remainder
synthesis
tech•niques
thē_authors
thē_end
tutorial

Adjectives

seminal
primary
explicit
implicit
unfamiliar
specialized
experimental
abstract

Adverbs

independently
solely

Preposition

Through

Other Useful Words

et al. [Latin] = and others

***Hints** on how to pronounce endings:*

1. ***–ed, –en*** *endings often include the flattened sound of* ***schwa, ə: ə + d*** *or* ***ə + n.***
2. ***Some –ed*** *endings have the sound,* ***[t].***
3. ***Use the long -ē sound to distinguish plural from singular on hypothesis, -es.***

(Rev. 09.11.20)

How to read a scientific paper critically

I. Dworkin, P. Romans* and A. Cordon

Apparently this document has been passed around campus [at U of T]. A student in ZOO357 this fall told me that it had proven itself useful in another course he had taken and suggested that we might make use of it as you prepare for the research article discussions. So here it is.

It is important that you develop the ability to read scientific articles critically. Although scientific articles represent a specialized form of writing, the critical faculties that you develop in reading the scientific literature will be useful to you in many areas of life. We expect that through careful reading, de-constructing and reconstructing selected research articles, you will enhance your critical reading skills considerably during the remainder of this course.

“Critical” does not necessarily mean negative. What critical reading does mean is that you will see beyond the “advertising” or “promotion” of one point of view to the central issues raised. You will also assess the data independently. It means that you will evaluate what has been presented and decide for yourself whether you agree with what has been asserted and to what extent.

NOT EVERYTHING YOU SEE IN PRINT IS NECESSARILY CORRECT OR TRUE.

Often when students start to read primary research papers they get frustrated because they try to understand all of the facts. And then they may get bogged down without seeing the main point of the paper. It is easy to get trapped in the detail especially when many of the terms are still new to you and the techniques are unfamiliar. In this document, we are presenting a more effective way for you to approach reading primary research papers. We believe that it will help you be a more critical reader faster. After all, you can't critically evaluate results if you do not see the main point of the work or the context within which it is written.

Let’s first start with a checklist of questions we can apply to the article by Ute Frevert *et al.* that you’ll be reading for the first discussion. These are general questions that you can then apply to all other papers we read in this course. For future papers and future tutorials, you should prepare for the tutorial by using this guide in reading the paper.

Then write down your comments and be prepared to share your findings and difficulties with the tutorial group.

1. Is there a major (big picture) question being addressed? If so, what is it?

2. Is there an hypothesis being tested? If so, what is it?

3. What (experimental) approaches are being taken to address the questions posed?

4. How should we interpret the results?

5. How are the results interpreted (by the authors) and how do they relate to the initial hypotheses and predictions?

6. What further experiments could be undertaken to answer questions only partly answered by the paper or new ones that arise because of the paper?

You might think that, in order to answer these questions, you should start reading at the beginning of the article and work straight through to the end. Few of us actually do this. Each scientist develops his or her own best way(s) to approach an article. These ways will depend, in part, on your purpose in reading it. For example, if you are primarily interested in a method used because you wish to use it yourself, you might only be interested in the parts of the paper that relate to that method. For purposes of this course, you will have to understand the paper in detail, but it may be best to start with the Abstract or Summary to get a perspective on the paper.

- A good Abstract will touch on all of the first 5 questions above, but depending on your familiarity with the subject, it may not be completely intelligible. It should certainly tell you whether the research reported in the article is likely to [be] relevant to a subject about which you are trying to gain knowledge.

- The Introduction section will elaborate on the context mentioned in the Abstract and give you a better idea "where the paper is going". Sometimes, at the end, it will even summarize the Results to be presented and the authors' conclusions, but be aware that this summary is really just advertising.

- If, after reading the Introduction, you still aren't sure what chief points are being addressed, you may want to go through the Discussion before reading the Results section. However doing so may cause you to restrict your thinking about the paper to the context that the authors are directing you towards. So, do this with caution.

- Move on to reading the Results section. You should definitely be skeptical of the authors' claims and conclusions until you are persuaded by the data presented in this section. One test of your abilities (and the authors' too) is whether you can reconstruct the paper solely from the data tables and figures.

- If you aren't familiar with the techniques used to obtain the data reported in the Results section, you should look carefully at the descriptions provided in the Materials and Methods section. This means that you may read by moving back and forth between these two sections, one set of experiments at a time. You might even have to consult some of the literature cited in the References section.

- Finally you should read the Discussion and then the Conclusions sections, or reread them if you have already read them.

Now is a good time to revisit the questions in greater detail:

1. Is there a major (big picture) question being addressed? If so, what is it?
    a. Are they trying to describe a phenomenon or provide a mechanistic explanation?
    b. Are there hypotheses relating to this question?
    c. Is this a seminal article in the area? (Does it provide synthesis, break new scientific ground or persuade you to change the way you think about the subject?)
    d. Is it a well-written paper or is it poorly put together? Did the authors make their work intelligible?

2. Is there an hypothesis being tested? If so, what is it?
    a. Does the hypothesis address the major question?
    b. What are the implicit or explicit assumptions underlying the hypothesis?
    c. What are the specific predictions made and do these predictions lead to tests of the hypothesis?

3. What (experimental) approaches are being taken [to] address the questions posed?
    a. What are the experiments?
    b. What is the rationale for each experiment?
    c. Should I go to another source (text book, review article, other literature cited in the article, the WEB, or the TA [consult the TA after you try other sources, you'll at least be able to refine your questions]) to get a better grasp of the methodology?
    d. Do the experiments really test the predictions?

4. How should I interpret the results?
    a. What are the controls and how do the experimental results differ from them?
    b. Do the results from each experiment make sense, that is, are they consistent?
    c. Are results from different experiments consistent with each other in providing support for the predictions they were designed to test?
    d. Are the results consistent with one or several hypotheses? Do they allow you to reject alternative hypotheses?

5. How are the results interpreted and how do they relate to the initial hypotheses and predictions?

    a. In the discussion, do you agree with the authors' interpretation of results? Why or why not?
    b. Are the limitations of the study and unresolved problems dealt with adequately?
    c. What does the article tell us that we didn't know before?

6. What experiments should be done for future follow-up? Do the authors suggest the same ones?

* * *

A Note on Citation: *These instructions contain extensive passages taken directly from a document prepared for ZOO329 by Ian Dworkin, now a professor at Michigan State, with suggestions from Prof. Ellen Larsen, and Anne Cordon, now at UTM. Prof. Romans edited, modified and expanded on their document for use in HMB321 and gave it back to them for use in other courses. This was **not** plagiarism because they were listed as co-authors, and because Dr. Romans did have permission to use the document as she saw fit....

[Editor's note: On her request, I've removed Prof. Larsen's name from the list of Authors. She writes that her contribution was too small. However, I retain this honorable mention.]

When you are writing about someone else's work, as you will be writing about work in the papers you read in this course, you must use your own words or else put the...words, phrases, sentences, etc. that you copy in quotation marks. You should also cite the original authors appropriately.

Statistics (V-6): Words 1469; s/p 1.8, w/s 16.3; passives 21%, FRE 59.5, GL 9.0

How to read – Critically! *Technical Writing, An Introduction* *2010.1.14, Edited by mns*

과학논문을 비판적으로 읽으려면* I. Dworkin, P. Romans, A. Cordon

과학논문을 비판적으로 읽는 능력을 기르는 일은 중요하다. 과학논문이 특수한 읽을 거리이긴 하지만 이 것을 읽는 동안에 길러진 비판력은 여러 일상생활에도 적용할 수 있기 때문이다. 선별한 논문을 주의깊게 읽고, 분석하고 재구성해보는 노력을 계속하다보면 비판적인 독서능력을 차츰 기르게 될 것이다.

여기서 '비판적'이란 말이 꼭 '부정적'이란 말을 뜻하는 건 아님을 유념해야 한다. 비판적으로 읽는다는 것은, 제기된 문제에 대하여 저자가 주장하는 하나의 관점에 독자가 얽매이지 않는 것을 말한다. 그러려면 저자가 제시한 데이터를 독자도 독립적으로 평가할 수 있어야 하며 저자의 주장을 어느 만큼 동의할 건지를 독자 스스로 판단할 수 있어야 한다.

인쇄물에 쓰인 내용이 모두 진리인 것은 아니다.

학생들이 무게있는 연구논문을 읽을 때에는 종종 난감함을 맛보게 되기도 하는데 그 이유는 논문에 적힌 내용을 모두 이해하려고 애쓰기 때문이다. 그러다 보면 수렁에 빠져서 글의 주된 논점을 놓치게 되고 마는 것이다. 특히 처음 듣는 용어들이 많거나 연구방법이 낯설 때에는 세부사항에 쉽게 붙들리고 만다. 이 글에서는 여러분이 논문을 읽는 더 효과적인 방법을 소개하고자 한다. 이 글대로 따라하다 보면 여러분도 비판적인 독자가 반드시 될 수 있다. 무엇보다 글의 주된 논점이나 글이 씌어진 문맥을 놓치고서는 논문의 결과를 비판적으로 평가할 수는 없게 된다는 점을 명심해야 한다.

논의를 시작하기에 앞서, 여러분이 읽게 될 특정 논문에 적용할 확인목록부터 언급해야겠다. 여러 질문들로 구성된 이 목록은 다른 논문을 읽을 때에도 적용할 수 있음은 물론이다. 먼저 아래에 제시한 목록을 준비하고 장차 논문을 읽은 후 각각의 질문에 답해야 함을 염두에 두도록 하라.

1. 논문에서 다루어진 주된 문제는 무엇인가?
2. 논문에서 검증하고자 하는 가설은 있는가? 있다면 무엇인가?
3. 논문에서 제기한 문제를 다루기 위하여 어떤 (실험) 방법이 사용되었는가?
4. 저자와는 별개로 여러분은 논문의 결과를 어떻게 설명하겠는가?**

*역자(이 원경)주: 여기서 '비판적으로'란 말은 강조하기 위해 사용한 것이기는 하지만 '불필요한 말이라고 볼 수도 있다. 왜냐하면 문헌을 비판적으로 읽지 않고는 창의적인 연구를 할 수는 없기 때문이다.

**역자주: 4 번과 5 번 질문의 순서에 유의하라. 저자의 설명을 묻기에 앞서서 독자가 결과를 어떻게 설명할 것인지를 왜 먼저 묻고 있는가?

5. 논문의 결과를 저자는 어떻게 설명하였으며 이 결과는 애초의 가설 혹은 예상과는 어떤 관련이 있는가?
6. 논문의 결과가 애초의 문제에 일부만 답한 경우 온전한 답을 얻기 위해서는 어떤 방법을 사용해야 하겠는가? 또한 이 논문 덕분에 새롭게 생겨난 문제를 다루기 위해서는 어떻게 해야 하겠는가?

여러분은, 이 질문들에 답하려면 논문을 처음부터 끝까지 쭉 읽어 나가야 하겠다고 생각할지 모르지만 반드시 그래야 하는 건 아니다. 모든 과학자들은 논문을 읽는 나름의 책략을 갖고 있다. 이 책략들은 부분적으론 논문을 읽는 목적에 따라 선택된다. 예를 들어, 여러분이 자신의 연구에서 사용해보기를 원하는 어떤 방법에만 주로 관심이 있다면, 읽고 있는 논문 안에서 그 방법과 관련된 부분에만 흥미를 갖게 될 것이다. 비록 위의 목록에 충실히 답하려면 논문을 자세히 이해해야 할 테지만, 논문의 대강을 알아보기 위해서는 초록이나 요약부터 시작하는 게 최선이다.

O 훌륭한 초록이라면 위의 목록의 처음 다섯가지 질문을 모두 다루고 있을 테지만 여러분이 해당 주제에 충분히 익숙하지 않은 경우, 초록을 완전히 이해하지는 못할 것이다. 다만 초록을 통해 이 논문에서 언급한 연구가 여러분이 정보를 얻고자 하는 주제와 관련이 있는지는 알 수 있어야 한다.

O 서론은 초록에서 언급한 내용을 더 자세히 설명하고 이 논문이 전개해 나갈 과정을 알려준다. 때로는 서론의 마지막에 결과와 결론의 요약을 담기도 하는데 이것은 독자의 흥미를 붙들어 두기 위한 것임을 알아 두어야 한다.

O 서론을 읽은 후에도 여전히 주된 논점을 알 수 없는 경우에는 결과를 건너 뛰어 토의*로 바로 가고 싶을 수도 있을 것이다. 이 경우엔 저자가 의도적으로 이끄는 방향으로 여러분의 사고가 제한될 수가 있으므로 조심해야 한다.
O 결과를 반드시 읽어보자. 여기서 제시되는 데이터를 통해 스스로 확인하기 전에는 저자의 주장과 결론을 반드시 의심해야만 한다. 논문에 제시된 데이터와 그림으로부터 논문의 결론을 재구성할 수 있을 때, 비로소 여러분의 능력이 (저자의 능력도) 검증되는 것이다**.

*역자주: 이 글은 논문이 초록, 서론, 본론(재료, 실험방법, 결과, 토의), 결론의 순서로 구성된 경우, 특히 실험논문을 예로 들고 있다.

**역자주: 논문에 제시된 데이터와 그림으로부터 독자가 독립적으로 내린 결론과, 저자의 결론이 일치하는지를 확인하기 전엔 저자를 믿지 말라는 뜻이다. 뿐만 아니라 유능한 독자로부터 검증받기 전엔 저자도 마음을 놓을 수가 없다는 말이다. 사실, 제대로 된 검증을 위해선 더 나아가서 저자가 제시한 데이터와 그림도 의심해 봐야 하는 것이다.

O 결과 부분에 주어진 데이터를 얻기 위해 저자가 사용한 방법에 익숙하지가 않으면 여러분은 재료 및 실험방법 부분에 제공된 설명을 주의깊게 살펴봐야 한다. 이 말은 한 번에 한 건의 실험을 검토하기 위해 이 두 부분을 앞뒤로 오가며 읽어야 함을 의미한다. 참고문헌에 인용된 논문도 살펴봐야 할지도 모른다.

O 끝으로 토의와 결론을 읽어야 한다. 이미 읽었다면 다시 읽어야 한다.

이젠 위의 목록의 질문들에 답하기 위해 질문들을 더 자세히 들여다 보자.

1. 논문에서 다루어진 주된 문제는 무엇인가?
   a. 저자는 하나의 현상을 제대로 설명하려고 하는가? 아니면 기계적인 설명만 제공하고 마는가?
   b. 이 질문과 관련한 가설이 있는가?
   c. 논문이 해당분야에서 장래성이 있는 논문인가? (논문이 종합적인 내용을 제공하거나 새로운 과학적 기반을 개척한 것인가? 아니면 해당주제에 대해 여러분이 이전에 지녀왔던 사고방식을 바꾸어 주는가?)
   d. 논문이 알기 쉽게 잘 씌어졌는가?

2. 논문에서 검증하고자 하는 가설은 있는가? 있다면 무엇인가?
   a. 이 가설이 주된 질문을 다루고 있는가?
   b. 이 가설의 기반이 되는, 드러나거나 숨어있는 가정은 무엇인가?
   c. 결과와 관련한 특별한 예상은 무엇이며 이 예상이 가설의 검증으로 이어지는가?

3. 논문에서 제기한 문제를 다루기 위하여 어떤 (실험) 방법이 사용되었는가?
   a. 실험내용은 어떤 것들로 구성되어 있는가?
   b. 각 실험의 이론적 근거는 무엇인가?
   c. 별개의 정보 출처에 의존해야하는가? (교과서, 논평논문, 참고문헌에 인용된 논문, 웹, 방법론을 더 잘 파악하기 위하여 전문가에게 문의 (단 이 때는 다른 자료를 먼저 충분히 검토하고 질문할 내용을 잘 정리한 후에 문의하는 게 좋다).)
   d. 실험 결과는 애초의 예상을 제대로 검증하는가?

4. 저자와는 별개로 여러분은 논문의 결과를 어떻게 설명하겠는가?
   a. 대조표준(실험적 관찰에서 소견을 비교하기 위한 표준)은 무엇이며 실험결과는 이들과 얼마나 다른가?
   b. 각각의 실험으로부터 얻은 결과들은 서로 일관성이 있는가?
   c. 다른 실험으로부터 얻은 결과들은 서로 일관성 있게 애초의 예상을 뒷받침하는 가?

d. 이 결과들은 하나 혹은 여러 가설과 일관성이 있는가? 이들은 대안으로 보였던 다른 가설을 배제하도록 도와주는가?

5. 논문의 결과를 저자는 어떻게 설명하였으며 이 결과는 애초의 가설 혹은 예상과는 어떤 관련이 있는가?
a. 토의부분에 주어진 결과에 대한 저자의 설명에 동의하는가? 왜 그런가?
b. 본 연구와 미해결 문제의 한계는 적절히 언급되었는가?
c. 논문은 전에 우리가 알지 못한 것에 대해 무엇을 말해주는가?

6. 논문의 결과가 애초의 문제에 일부만 답한 경우 온전한 답을 얻기 위해서는 어떤 방법을 사용해야 하겠는가? 또한 이 논문 덕분에 새롭게 생겨난 문제를 다루기 위해서는 어떻게 해야 하겠는가?

역자: 이원경, 교수 *Translated into Korean by Prof. Lee, Won Kyoung, 2009.5.19*

Editor's Note: My thanks to Professor Lee, Won Kyoung for his thoughtful translation of this widely accepted article, especially since he strongly disagrees with the order of ideas and, indeed, the whole pedagogical method it presents. Each reader must find his own best path to better understanding of professional or technical papers. *mns*

Advanced Academic Writing

Proofread & Re-write

Here is an exact excerpt from an actual paper written for professional publication:

[TITLE?]

Methods : We compared the blood static pattern and symptoms according to The Diagnostic Criteria for Blood stasis Syndrome between patient group 38 patients(male 18, female 20) that admitted due to acute cerebral infarction within 7days after stroke attack in Dept. of Internal Medicine, [City] Oriental Medicine Hospital from August 2001 to June 2002 and control group, 36 patients(male 17, female 19) that had described normal state without a history of storke(included Transient Ischemic Stroke) through the health examination from April 2002 to June 2002.

Results and Conclusions : In the blood static pattern, the patient group was more severer than the control group. We could find significant difference in....

Exercise A: Proofreading Instructions

1. Consider <u>only</u> the first paragraph on **Methods.**
2. Count the number of words _____ and sentences _____.
3. What's the <u>average</u> number of words per sentence in paragraph one? ______.
4. What is the average number of words per sentence we try to achieve? ______.
5. So, about how many sentences do we need, to tell all this information? ___ or ___.

Exercise B: Discuss and re-write the "Methods" section

1) Who is writing this article? 2) Why do people write research papers?

3) What word-processing tools did this writer FAIL to USE? How do you know that?

4) Three groups of people participated in this research. Name them.

5) Why did people in each of these three groups come to the hospital?

6) Write two sentences to describe each of the two <u>patient</u> groups.

7) What is the key difference between these two groups?

8) Give this professional article an informative <u>title</u>.

Now, re-write the paragraph on Methods on the following page. Write short, factual statements using active verbs. Tell the research "story" clearly. Can the result still be professional? **<u>Optional:</u>** Word-process your new version. How many people can read and understand this research report, now that you have re-written it for that purpose?

Exercise Statistics: words 199; s/p 2.0, w/s 8.5; passives 0%, reading ease 72.4, grade level 5.2

Proofread & Re-write, Exercise © mns   Technical Writing, An Introduction   Rev.2009.11, 2009.2; 15/11/02

[TITLE?]

We studied two groups of people. The first group included…

Fair Use

http://www.copyright.gov/fls/fl102.html

One of the rights accorded to the owner of copyright is the right to reproduce or to authorize others to reproduce the work in copies or phonorecords. This right is subject to certain limitations found in sections 107 through 118 of the Copyright Act (title 17, U. S. Code). One of the more important limitations is the doctrine of "fair use." Although fair use was not mentioned in the previous copyright law, the doctrine has developed through a substantial number of court decisions over the years. This doctrine has been codified in section 107 of the copyright law.

Section 107 contains a list of the various purposes for which the reproduction of a particular work may be considered "fair," such as criticism, comment, news reporting, teaching, scholarship, and research. Section 107 also sets out four factors to be considered in determining whether or not a particular use is fair:

1. the purpose and character of the use, including whether such use is of commercial nature or is for nonprofit educational purposes;
2. the nature of the copyrighted work;
3. amount and substantiality of the portion used in relation to the copyrighted work as a whole; and
4. the effect of the use upon the potential market for or value of the copyrighted work.

The distinction between "fair use" and infringement may be unclear and not easily defined. There is no specific number of words, lines, or notes that may safely be taken without permission. Acknowledging the source of the copyrighted material does not substitute for obtaining permission.

The 1961 *Report of the Register of Copyrights on the General Revision of the U.S. Copyright Law* cites examples of activities that courts have regarded as fair use: "quotation of excerpts in a review or criticism for purposes of illustration or comment; quotation of short passages in a scholarly or technical work, for illustration or clarification of the author's observations; use in a parody of some of the content of the work parodied; summary of an address or article, with brief quotations, in a news report; reproduction by a library of a portion of a work to replace part of a damaged copy; reproduction by a teacher or student of a small part of a work to illustrate a lesson; reproduction of a work in legislative or judicial proceedings or reports; incidental and fortuitous reproduction, in a newsreel or broadcast, of a work located in the scene of an event being reported."

Copyright protects the particular way an author has expressed himself; it does not extend to any ideas, systems, or factual information conveyed in the work.

The safest course is always to get permission from the copyright owner before using copyrighted material. The Copyright Office cannot give this permission.

When it is impracticable to obtain permission, use of copyrighted material should be avoided unless the doctrine of "fair use" would clearly apply to the situation. The Copyright Office can neither determine if a certain use may be considered "fair" nor advise on possible copyright violations. If there is any doubt, it is advisable to consult an attorney.

FL-102, Revised July 2006

U.S. Copyright Office
101 Independence Avenue SE
Washington, DC 20559-6000
(202) 707-3000

PART 13 - WRITING IS A TECHNOLOGY

Five Hundred Years of Printing (Illustration)

Writing Is A Technology (An Essay in English)

► Assignment – Find The Key Points (Class Exercise)

Hūnminjeongeum, Proclaimed 1446 (Illustration)

۞ 글쓰기는 기술이다.

Revised Romanization, Proclaimed July 7, 2000

Modern Hangul Characters

UNESCO/ Jikji Memory of the World Prize

Teaching Points:

Find Key Ideas in Summaries and Abstracts

A Brief History of Writing and Printing

Koreans' Leading Role in Print Technology

Five Hundred Years of Printing

S. H. Steinberg

500 years of Printing

500 years of Printing

500 years of Printing

500 years of Printing

500 years of Printing

500 years of Printing

500 years of PRINTING

500 years of Printing

500 years of Printing

WRITING IS A TECHNOLOGY

By Michael Neil Shapiro

Writing is a major human technology. It is the memory of the human race. It is an evolving technology. Koreans have historically been leaders in developing such technologies. We can and should benefit from the best writing technology available. Writing technologies depend upon established customs and forms. Our task is to master standard writing customs, methods and editing tools. We have been doing so by applying our new knowledge to specific writing tasks.

WRITING is a TECHNOLOGY. It's one of the earliest and still most powerful technologies of mankind. It is our collective memory—the memory of the human race. It permits accurate, long-term storage of data and ideas. It is as valuable to human success as the use of fire or the invention of the wheel.

Writing is an evolving technology. It has evolved in both the tools we use (hardware) and in the methods, "rules", customs and symbols (software) that we use to record our ideas. In early days, people wrote in sand, with sticks, or painted on rocks. Then we engraved pictures and words in rock surfaces. A teen-age boy with a pocket-knife may still carve "John loves Mary" in the bark of a tree. The tools are relatively simple, but the results are NOT PORTABLE.

If you press a pointed tool into a cake of wet clay (a special mud) and let it dry in the sun, you have a fairly permanent record that can be carried and stored. This storage could be the beginning of a library. Roman school children "wrote" their lessons on wax tablets with a pointed metal stick, called a *stylus.*[1] At the end of the day, their lessons were melted away to prepare for the next day's classes. (Perhaps this process is not so different from modern students' experience, after all!)

Then came animal skins, papyrus and paper to write on. The writing was done with ink, applied with brushes, sharpened birds' feathers, metal points, little ball-bearings and now nylon tips. Scholars young and old have also used thin graphite cores inserted in wood or plastic sleeves. We call them pencils. All these are tools for "handwriting". Among great classics in any language, a great many have been written by hand. This is sometimes true even today.[2]

Between the years 1443-1446, King Sejong the Great of Korea developed a new system for writing the Korean language. He called it *Hūnminjeongeum,* or "Proper Sound to Instruct the People." This system is a masterpiece of bio-mechanical observation, plus an elegantly simple system of transcription. Letters represent individual sounds <u>and</u> the mouth positions for making them. Letters are made of just two graphic elements, a "ball" and a "stick", a zero and a one.[3] Complex sounds are made by combining several such

---

[1] The word "stylus" is a Latin word that also described the "needle" used to play music recorded on old vinyl disks, rotating at 33, 45 or even 78 rpm. These disks were called "records". Another, "stylus" was used to create the original, master disk, from which perhaps millions of copies were later pressed.

[2] J. K. Rowling began writing *Harry Potter* by hand, finished her manuscript for *Harry Potter and the Philosopher's Stone* on an old manual typewriter, and now operates an official website, using a computer. (She can afford several.) Sources: *en.wikipedia.org/wiki/JK_Rowling* and published interviews.

[3] It seems to me this writing method may be a very early example of binary (or digital?) code. Samuel Morse developed his telegraphic code—"an early form of digital code" in the early 1840's (Wikipedia). In

elements. Syllables, or pronounceable units, are written in individual blocks, usually containing two, three or four letters, combined according to a few established rules.

At about the same time, clever, determined men, East and West, developed the technologies of casting metal type and setting the pieces into page-size matrices to make multiple copies of books. *Voilà,* the technologies of typesetting and printing were born! Korean artisans, craftsmen and engineers were leaders and innovators in printing, among other technologies, even centuries ago. [4] Then, especially in the 1800's to 1900's, machines were developed so that individuals could create a page of "printed" writing themselves, at home or in the office. And "typewriters" speeded commerce. Then, in the 1960's to 80's, typewriters were made using electric power. Speed increased again. Today we still use some of those earlier tools and technologies. Can I borrow your pen?

But all that was true "B.C.", that is, "Before Computers." Now we can create and save documents electronically. We can print them quickly at home or in the office. For temporary storage and portability of documents, we have had "floppy disks" (diskettes). Then came recordable CD's for more permanent recording of much more and varied material, including music, books and photographs. Now, students or professors can carry the whole semester's notes, and even presentations, "written" electronically on little USB "memory" devices hanging around their necks, or decorating their mobile phones. And we can send documents and messages to any part of the world at electronic speed.

The technologies of written communication are evolving faster and faster. But they could not exist at all without standard methods and protocols[5] for both hardware and software. Computers use grammars and logic much stricter than those of ordinary human language. But human languages, verbal and mathematical, are the basis for all later technologies.

Over centuries, people have developed standard methods, customs and conventions for managing their languages. One requirement in any "language" course, including mathematics or computers, is to master the **basic grammar.** In verbal language, "grammar" means the logic of sentence structure. Good writing requires good **punctuation**—proper use of the "traffic signals" that guide our eyes and our understanding through any written page.

We can and should benefit from the newest writing and editing technologies available in our computers. These include spelling and grammar checking tools, and word and sentence counting tools. The Microsoft Word writing program also offers us a readability

---

Korea, "the people" are now almost universally literate. The use of Hangeul for over 550 years might help to explain the early, avid and "ubiquitous" acceptance of computers in modern Korean society, A.D. I've also noticed that Hangeul is more efficient than English in storing contact information in my mobile phone.

[4] In the West, Johannes Gutenberg, in Mainz, Germany used his printing press to produce the first copies of the Christian Bible printed with movable metal type (1455). In the East, at Heungdeoksa Temple, Cheongju City, Korea, priests developed printing with movable metal type to make copies of a Zen (Seon) Buddhist text. The 'Jikji' was printed in 1377, 78 years before the Gutenberg Bible. It is interesting that the UNESCO Jikji Prize, created in 2004, carries the sub-title, "Memory of the World."

[5] **Protocol** *n.,* [definition #] **7.** a set of rules governing the format of messages that are exchanged between computers. *[Random House Webster's College Dictionary, pp. 1064-5]*

statistics calculator. Computers are wonderful calculators. We can and should use all of these available tools to improve the quality of our writing, immediately and remarkably.

Our task in a Technical Writing course is to master established writing customs and forms, standard methods and editing tools. We have been doing so by applying our new knowledge to a variety of specific writing tasks: making concise summaries; designing and editing good job application letters; sending proper e-mails, analyzing product manuals, and wrestling with editing excerpts of actual articles written for professional publication.

Journalists use the same tools and skills to write catchy news headlines. Marketers and advertisers devise promotional articles and advertisements.

You can never solve in school every problem you will ever face in life. What you CAN do is learn reliable methods and skills, standard tools and techniques. These you can apply to whatever specific situation, demand or task comes your way.

Summary of the main points:

1) Writing is a major human technology.
2) It is the memory of the human race.
3) It is an evolving technology.
4) Koreans have historically been leaders in developing such technologies.
5) We can and should benefit from the best writing technology available.
6) Writing technologies depend upon established customs and forms.
7) Our task is to master standard writing customs, methods and editing tools.
8) We have been doing so by applying our new knowledge to specific writing tasks.

Statistics (Summary): Words 78; words/sentence 13.1; Readability: passives 0%, Flesch Reading Ease 48.0, Grade Level 8.8

REFERENCES

NOTE: A complete academic paper would have references attached on the last pages. The author has omitted the list of references here, for TWO reasons:

1. **The teaching focus of this lesson** is on finding the key ideas of an academic paper in the Abstract and/or Introduction, ***or*** in the Summary and/or Conclusions.

2. **The style of references to use** is also a technical matter of concern. For this essay, the MLA (Modern Language Association) style of reference is appropriate.

   However, since most students enrolled in this course are Mechanical Engineers, the proper reference style is the "scientific" or APA style, sponsored by the American Psychological Association.

Students should also find and examine references in their various course textbooks.

Statistics (net): Words 1237; s/p 3.1, words/sentence 13.1; Readability: passives 7%, Flesch Reading Ease 51.2, Grade Level 9.3

"Writing Is A Technology"

How to Read an Academic Essay Efficiently

Assignment—Find the Key Points

Instructions:

A. You may do this assignment alone, or with a partner.

B. Write a list of key points for this essay. Use the lines numbered 1 to 8 below.

HINT: DO NOT read the whole essay. Just find the key points. Then write them down.

C. Where's the best place to look for this key information? Complete the sentence below:

The best place to look is at the __________________, in the _________________

or at the _____________, in the ___________________ or ____________________.

D. Give this list a good, clear **title**. Put your title on the line below. Try to center it.

[HINT: What is this list?]

____

[Title]

1. ____
2. ____
3. ____
4. ____
5. ____
6. ____
7. ____
8. ____

Note: This is an exercise in working smart before you work hard. Working smart & hard is best.

Now, I invite you to read the whole essay. It is available in English and in Korean.

Statistics (V-21): Words 160; s/p 2.0, w/s 7.5; passives 0%, FRE 96.9, GL 1.5

Assignment: Writing is a Tech *Technical Writing, An Introduction* *2009.2 (2007) © mns*

Hūnminjeongum, 1446

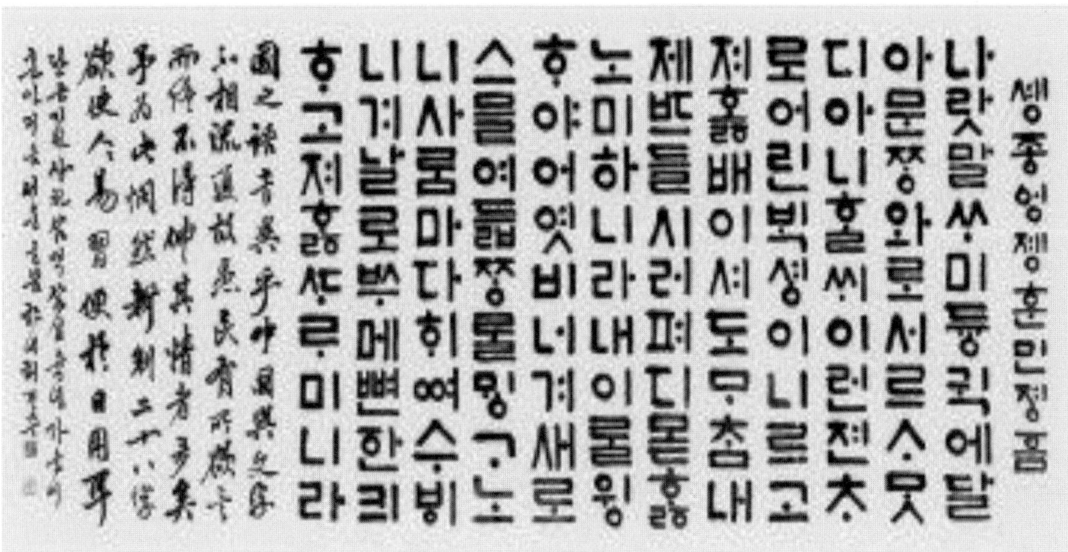

http://d.seoche.co.kr/data/gallery/r/tmb6_r061218105050055.jpg

훈 민 정 음

"Teach the People the Proper Sounds."

글쓰기는 기술이다.

글쓰기는 주된 인간의 기술이다. 글쓰기는 인류의 기억이며, 진화하는 기술이다. 한국인들은 역사적으로 이런 기술을 발전시키는데 있어서 선도자들이었다. 우리는 최선의 글쓰기 실력으로부터 이득을 얻을 수 있으며 또한 그렇게 해야 한다. 글쓰기 기술은 잘 확립된 요령들과 양식에 따라 좌우된다. 우리의 임무는 표준 글쓰기 요령, 방법 및 편집 도구 등을 잘 익히는 것이다. 우리는 글쓰기에 관련한 새로운 지식을 특정한 과제에 적용함으로써 그러한 요령, 방법, 도구 등을 익혔다.

글쓰기는 기술이다. 작문은 인류에게 가장 일찍이 존재했었으며, 현재도 가장 강력한 기술중의 하나이다. 글쓰기는 우리의 총체적인 기억, 즉 인류의 기억이다.
글쓰기는 정확하고, 장기적인 데이터와 사고들을 가능케 한다. 글쓰기는 인류의 성공에 있어서 불의 사용이나 바퀴의 발명만큼이나 값어치가 있는 기술이다.

글쓰기는 진화하는 기술이다. 우리가 사용하는 도구(하드웨어)와 우리의 생각들을 기록한 방법, 규칙, 습성 및 기호 등(소프트웨어) 모두가 진화한다. 옛날에는 사람들은 모래 위에 나무 막대기로 글을 쓰거나 바위에 그림을 그렸다. 그 이후에, 사람들은 바위에 그림이나 글씨를 새겼다. 10 대의 소년이 주머니 칼로 "John 은 Mary 를 사랑해" 라고 나무 껍질에 새길 수도 있다. 도구는 상대적으로 간단하지만, 결과는 절대로 옮겨질 수 없다.

끝이 뾰족한 도구로 찰흙에 무엇인가를 새긴 후, 햇빛에 말리면, 당신은 꽤 영원히 간직하고 가지고 다닐 수 있는 기록을 갖게 된다. 이 기록물이 도서관의 시작이 될 수도 있다. 로마의 학교 어린이들은 그들이 배운 가르침을 왁스로 만든 판에 스타일러스[1] 라는 뾰족한 금속 막대기로 적었다. 그리고 그날 밤에 그들이 배운 내용을 다음날을 위해 녹여 없앴다. (아마도 이러한 과정은 현대의 학생들의 경험에 비추어도 별로 다를 것이 없을 것이다.)

그리고는 동물의 피부, 파피루스 및 종이가 전래되었다. 글쓰기는 잉크로 써졌으며, 붓, 뾰쪽하게 만든 새의 깃털, 금속, 작은 볼 베어링 및 현재의 나일론 팁 같은 것들이 사용되었다. 어리거나 나이든 학자들은 나무나 플라스틱 통에 얇은 흑연 막대기를 넣은 것을 사용해 왔다. 우리는 이것을 연필이라 부른다. 이런 모든 도구들은 손으로 글을 쓰기 위한 도구들이다. 어느 언어에서건 많은 훌륭한 고전들이 손으로 쓰여졌다. 오늘날에도 때때로 그러한 경우가 있다.[2]

1443 년부터 1446 년 사이에, 세종대왕은 한국어를 위한 새로운 시스템을 개발했다. 세종대왕은 이를 "훈민정음" 혹은 "국민을 가르치기 위한 적절한 소리"라 명명했다. 이 시스템은 생체역학적 관찰의 걸작이면서도, 우아하고도 매우 간결한 표현 방식이다. 문자들은 각각의 소리들과 그 소리들을 만들기 위한 입 모양을 표현한다. 문자들은 단지 두 개의 도해적 요소로 구성되어 있다. "하나의 점" 과 "막대기", 즉 영과 일[3]. 복잡한

---

[1] "stylus" 는 라틴어로 바늘을 의미하며, 음악용 레코드 판을 읽을 때 쓰는 바늘을 부르는 말이다. 또 다른 예로는 원본, 마스터 디스크를 만들 때 사용되는 단어이다. 마스터 디스크로부터 나중에 많은 복사본이 단지 눌려지는 방법에 의해 복사된다.

[2] J. K. Rowling 은 *Harry Potter* 를 손으로 쓰기 시작했고, *Harry Potter 와 the Philosopher's Stone* 을 오래된 수동 타이프 라이터로 그녀의 원고를 끝냈다. 그러나 지금은 컴퓨터를 이용하여 공식 웹사이트를 운영한다. Sources: *en.wikipedia.org/wiki/JK_Rowling* and published interviews.

[3] 필자에게는 이러한 문자 표현 방법은 매우 오래된 이진법 코드(또는 디지털)로 보인다. 사뮤엘 모오스는 원격 문자 코드를 개발했다- 1840 년대 초반에 "초기 형태의 디지털 코드". 한국의 국민들은 거의 대부분 글을 읽고 쓸 줄 안다. 550 년 이상 한글의 사용이 현대 한국 사회의 급속적인 컴퓨터의 전국보급현상을

소리들은 그 와 같은 몇 개의요소들로 만들어 진다. 음절, 즉 소리단위는 개별적 묶음으로 씌어졌고, 대체로 2 개, 3 개 또는 4 개의 문자들로 구성되어 있으며, 적절한 규칙에 따라 조합되어 있다.

거의 같은 시기에, 훌륭한 동서양의 사람들이 금속 활자 기술을 개발하여, 활자들을 한 페이지 크기의 배열로 만든 다음 여러 권의 책을 만들 수 있게 하였다. 자 보라, 활자배치 기술과 인쇄술이 태어났다! 인쇄술에 있어서 한국의 장인들과 기술자들은, 다른 기술들 중에서도, 특히 몇 백 년 전에는, 선구자였으며 혁신적인 개발자들이었다.[4] 그 이후에, 특히, 1800 년대에서 1900 년대 사이에 기계가 개발되었고, 개개인들이 집이나 사무실에서 자신의 글을 인쇄된 형태로 만들어 낼 수 있게 되었다. 그리고 "타이프라이터(typewriters)"는 상업을 가속화 시켰다. 그리고, 1960 년대부터 80 년대에 타이프 라이터는 전기를 이용하여 동작하도록 만들어 져서, 인쇄 속도가 더욱 증가하게 되었다. 오늘날 우리는 여전히 초기단계의 도구나 기술들을 사용하기도 한다.

그러나 이런 것들은 컴퓨터 개발이전의 이야기이다. 우리는 지금 문서를 전자적으로 만들어 내고 저장할 수 있으며, 우리는 이 문서들을 집이나 사무실에서 빠르게 인쇄할 수 있다. 문서의 임시 저장이나 이동성을 위해서, "플로피 디스크"(디스켓) 가 있었고, 후에 좀더 영구적이며 더 많은 양을 저장해 두기 위한 "저장 가능한 CD"가 개발되었으며, 이런 매체에는 음악, 책, 사진 등 다양한 자료들이 저장되었다. 오늘날에는 학생들이나 교수들이 한 학기 분량의 강의 노트나 심지어는 발표 자료를 작은 USB 메모리에 담아 목걸이처럼 걸고 다니거나 핸드폰 장식품으로 달고 다닌다. 그리고 우리는 문서나 메시지를 전세계 어디에나 전기의 속도로 보낼 수 있다.

글쓰기를 통한 의사소통기술은 점점 더 빠르게 진화하고 있다. 하지만, 이러한 의사소통기술은 하드웨어와 소프트웨어간의 통신규약(Protocol[5]) 과 표준 방법 없이는 전혀 이루어 질 수 없다. 컴퓨터는 문법과 논리를 일반적인 사람들이 사용하는 말 보다 훨씬 엄격하게 적용한다. 그러나 인간의 언어는, 구두로 하거나 수치적으로 하거나, 모두 최근 기술을 토대로 하고 있다.

수세기에 걸쳐서, 인류는 자신들의 언어를 다루는 표준 방식, 습관 및 관습을 개발해 왔다. 수학이나 컴퓨터를 포함한 어떤 언어 교과에 있어서 하나의 요구사항은 기본 문법을 마스터 하라는 것이다. 구어에 있어서, "문법"이란 문장 구조의 논리를 의미한다. 글을 잘 쓰기 위해서는 필요한 문장부호를 잘 활용 할 줄 알아야 한다. 다시 말하면, 어떤 페이지를 읽더라도 우리의 눈과 이해력을 이끌어줄 "교통 신호"를 적절히 넣을 줄 알아야 한다.

우리는 컴퓨터에서 사용할 수 있는 가장 최신의 글쓰기와 편집기술로부터 도움을 받을 수 있어야 하고 받아야만 한다. 이는 철자와 문법 검토 기능과 단어 수 및 문장 수를

설명하는데 도움이 될 것 같다. 더욱이, 필자는 이미 한글이 핸드폰에서 영어보다 더 효율적이라는 점을 인식했다

[4] 서양에서는, 독일 마인지방의 Johannes Gutenberg 가 이동 가능한 금속활자로 구성된 자신의 인쇄기를 사용하여 성경을 처음으로 찍어내었다.(1455) 동양에서는 한국의 청주에 있는 흥덕사에서, 성직자(스님)들이 이동 가능한 금속활자를 개발하여 선종 불교 교리를 인쇄하였다. '직지심경'은 1377 년에 인쇄되었으며, Guttenberg 의 성경보다 78 년 앞선 인쇄 기록이다. 2004 년에 유네스코가 직지상을 제정하면서 "전세계의 기념물(Memory of the World)" 이라고 부제를 달은 것은 흥미로운 일이다."

[5] **Protocol** *n.*, [definition #] **7. 컴퓨터상에서 정보를 교환하는 양식의 종합적 통신규약** *[Random House Webster's College Dictionary, pp. 1064-5]*

세어주는 기능 등을 포함한다. Microsoft Word 프로그램은 또한 문장의 통계 계산기능을 제공한다. 컴퓨터는 훌륭한 계산기이다. 우리는, 바로 지금 또한 상당 수준, 이런 모든 확보 가능한 도구들을 우리가 쓴 글의 질을 향상시키기 위하여 사용할 수 있어야만 한다. Technical writing course 에서 우리의 과제는 확립된 글쓰기 관습과 양식, 표준적인 방법 및 편집 도구들을 습득하는 것이다. 우리는 우리의 새로운 지식들을 적용해서 여러 가지 특정 글쓰기 과제에의 적용, 간결한 요약문 작성, 취업 지원서 작성 및 편집, 적절한 e-mail 보내기, 생산제품 설명서 분석 및 전문적인 출판을 위해 쓰여진 실제 문건의 편집 전문가와 맞붙어 경쟁해 봄으로써 이 과정의 목표를 달성하였다.

저널리스트들은 같은 도구와 기술들을 사용해서 사람들의 마음을 끄는 뉴스 표제를 작성한다. 마케팅 담당자들과 광고자들은 판촉을 위한 문구와 광고물들을 고안해 낸다.

당신은 인생에서 언젠가 만나게 될 모든 문제를 학교에서 해결할 수는 없다. 당신이 할 수 있는 것은 믿을 만한 방법과 기술 및 표준적인 도구들과 기술들을 배워두는 것이다. 어떠한 상황이 오더라도 당신이 적용할 수 있는 이러한 요구나 과제들은 당신이 가는 길에 도움이 될 것이다.

<u>핵심요점</u>:

1) 글쓰기는 인간의 주된 기술 이다.
2) 글쓰기는 인류의 기록이다.
3) 글쓰기는 진화하는 기술이다.
4) 한국인은 역사적으로 이러한 기술들에 있어서 선구자였다.
5) 우리는 얻을 수 있는 가장 좋은 글쓰기도구들로부터 도움을 받아야 한다.
6) 글쓰기 기술은 확립된 관습과 형식을 따르게 된다.
7) 우리의 임무는 표준 글쓰기 관습, 방법 및 편집 도구들을 익히는 것이다.
8) 우리는 여러 가지 특정 글쓰기 과제에의 적용 등을 통해서 이를 달성하였다.

참고문헌

<u>NOTE</u>: 완전한 학문적 논문목록은 마지막 페이지에 나와있다. 여기에 참고문헌을 적지 않는 두 가지 이유는 다음과 같다.

1. 이 학과목 과정의 집중교육부분은 초록이나 서론부분, 혹은 요약문, 결론 부분에서 학술 논문의 핵심을 찾아내는 것이다.
2. 사용하고자 하는 참고문헌의 형식 또한 관심사항의 기술 적인 문제이다. 현재의 글에서는 MLA(Modern Language Association: 현대 언어 협회) 형식의 참고문헌이 적절하다고 생각된다.
   하지만, 이 학과목 수강 학생 대부분이 기계공학과 학생들이기 때문에, 적절한 참고문헌 형식은 "과학" 또는 미국 심리 학회의 지원을 받는 APA 형태가 될 것이다.

학생들은 또한 다양한 교과목 교재의 참고문헌들을 찾아보고 검토해 보아야 한다.

Revised Romanization of Korean

From Wikipedia, the free encyclopedia

The **Revised Romanization of Korean** is the official Korean language romanization system in South Korea. It is the official South Korean replacement for the 1984 McCune-Reischauer–based romanization system. The new system is similar to the older system, but eliminates diacritics and is more closely based on Korean phonology than on western perception of Korean phonetics.

The Revised Romanization uses no non-alphabetic symbols except very limited, often optional, use of the hyphen. It was developed by the National Academy of the Korean Language from 1995 and was released to the public on July 7, 2000, by South Korea's Ministry of Culture and Tourism in Proclamation No. 2000-8. The proclamation included the following reasons for the new system:[1]

> It is convenient to type on computers since it uses only Latin letters and symbols, omitting the apostrophes and breves that were problematic with the McCune-Reischauer system.
>
> It promotes consistent romanization by native Korean speakers by better transcribing important language characteristics.
>
> It reduces the confusion caused by the tendency to ignore apostrophes and diacritics.
>
> It rationalizes the Korean language with the plain ASCII text of internet domain names.

References

1. ^ [a] [b] Ministry of Culture & Tourism: *The Revised Romanization of Korean* (July 2000). Retrieved on 2007-05-09.

Korean Language Practice

About Hangul | Writing | Phrases | Vocabulary

The **Korean language** is classified as a member of the Ural-Altaic family (other members of this family include the Mongolian, Finnish, and Hungarian languages.) Until the early 1400s, most documents were written in classical Chinese characters (known in Korean as *Hanja*). As the idiographs are difficult to learn, only the educated people could read and write. King Sejong, the 4th ruler of the Joseon dynasty (1392-1910), set up a special committee of scholars in 1443 to create a new writing system specifically suited to the Korean language.

The result was *Hangul* (meaning 'the one script'). It originally contained 28 symbols, although 4 have dropped out of use. The alphabet has 10 vowels and 14 consonants. The consonants represent the simplified outlines of the parts of the mouth and tongue used to pronounce them. The vowels are associated with elements of the philosophy of the *Book of Changes*.

In 1994, Discovery magazine described *Hangul* as the most logical language writing system in the world. The simplicity of *Hangul* led Korea to become one of the most literate countries in the world. U.S. novelist Pearl Buck said that *Hangul* is the simplest writing system in the world and likened *King Sejong* to Leonardo da Vinci. Even though *Hangul* is a system of phonetic symbols, it is categorized as new level of feature system, the first and the only in the world. On Oct. 1, 1997, UNESCO designated *Hunminjeongeum* as world archive property. Koreans commemorate the creation of *Hangul* each year on October 9.

The *Hangul* Characters

●Consonants:

ㄱ	ㄴ	ㄷ	ㄹ	ㅁ	ㅂ	ㅅ	ㅇ	ㅈ
\k,g\	\n\	\t,d\	\r,l\	\m\	\p,b\	\s,sh\	\ng\	\ch,j\
kiyok	niun	tikut	riul	mium	piup	siot	iung	chiut

ㅊ	ㅋ	ㅌ	ㅍ	ㅎ
\ch'\	\k'\	\t'\	\p',f\	\h\
ch'iut	k'iuk	t'iut	p'iup	hiut

●Vowels

ㅏ	ㅑ	ㅓ	ㅕ	ㅗ	ㅛ	ㅜ	ㅠ	ㅡ	ㅣ
\a\	\ya\	\eo\	\yeo\	\o\	\yo\	\u\	\yu\	\eu\	\ee\

http://www.lifeinkorea.com/Language/korean.cfm *[Page 1 only, here, of 2]*

News

Communication and Information Sector's news service

2007 Jikji Prize awarded to Austria's Phonogrammarchiv

11-09-2007 (Paris)

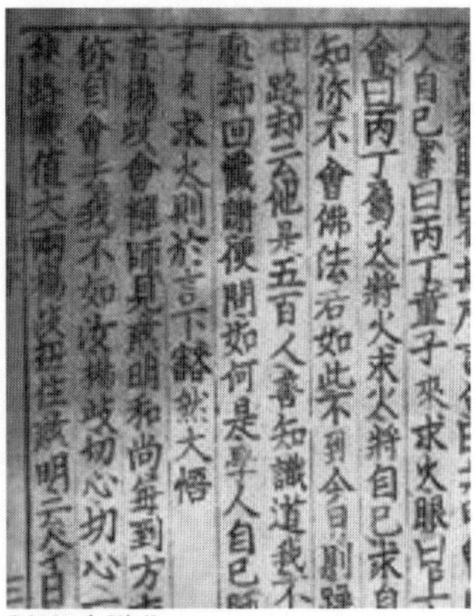

Digital Jikji

In an impressive ceremony held on 4 September 2007 in Cheongju City, in the Republic of Korea, the Phonogrammarchiv of the Austrian Academy of Sciences formally received the UNESCO/Jikji Memory of World Prize certificate and cheque.

The ceremony was held at the Grand Hall of the Cheongju Arts Centre for some 1,200 specially invited participants. Previously recorded congratulatory video messages were delivered by UNESCO's Director-General, Mr Koïchiro Matsuura, and the Secretary-General of the United Nations, Mr Ban Ki-Moon, in addition to speeches delivered by the Minister of Culture, the Governor of Chungcheungbukdo Province and the Mayor of Cheongju City.

Participants were treated to cultural performances of Korean groups in music and dance.

The UNESCO/Jikji Memory of World Prize, the first prize in the field of documentary heritage, was established by UNESCO in April 2004 to commemorate the inscription of Jikji, the oldest surviving book made with moveable metal characters, on the Memory of World Register.

The Prize, consisting of an award of US$30,000, along with a certificate, is given every two years to individuals or institutions that have made a significant contribution to the preservation and accessibility of the documentary heritage.

The National Library of the Czech Republic was the first recipient of the 2005 UNESCO/Jikji Memory of the World Prize. Recognition received through the Prize greatly helped to initiate several important activities and to expand the scope of its ongoing work. It also led to closer cooperation with a number of other institutions outside Europe, such as the National Library of China and the National Library of Kazakhstan, but more importantly, it also fostered new forms of cooperation with the National Library of the Republic of Korea in Seoul and with the Early Printing Museum in Cheongju.

This year's winner, the Phonogrammarchiv, is the oldest sound archive in the world, having been founded in 1899. It has made a substantial contribution to the advancement of audiovisual preservation and it plans to use the prize money to assist in preserving a collection in a developing country.

Jikji certificate being received by the Phonogrammarchiv
© UNESCO

http://portal.unesco.org/ci/en/ev.php

PART – 14 SUPPORTING STUDENTS' SUCCESS

Day One Revisited - Course Goals & Two Secrets

۞ 시험을 잘 치기 위한 요령

Tips for Taking Exams

EQUILIBRIUM - or, The Keys to the Kingdom, Homage to Rudolf Flesch

From Wikipedia, the free encyclopedia

ISS – International Space Station

After STS-120 in November 2007

Day One Revisited
COURSE GOALS & TWO SECRETS
Technical Writing

Goals for My Students

1. Pass the course.
2. Get a good grade.
3. Write well in English.

Rev. 12 Feb 08 *Please post these student goals where you will see them often.*

Academic Goal

The academic goal of this course is
to produce effective writing by conscious design.

Sentence Statistics: words 14; w/s 14; passives 0%, Flesch reading ease 53.6, grade level 9.2

Academic Goal (V-13) *Technical Writing, An Introduction* *2009.2 (2008)*

Two Secrets to Writing Well

1. **Read a lot. By reading, you will learn what good writing looks like.**

2. **Practice writing, editing, and re-writing. "Practice makes perfect."**

Statistics (Rev. 7): Words 26; w/s 5.2; Readability: Passives 0 %, Reading Ease 76.6, Grade Level 3.8

Overall Statistics: words 126; w/s 6.3; passives 0%, Flesch reading ease 80.1, grade level 3.6

Day One, Combined Info *Technical Writing, An Introduction* *2009.6 © mns*

시험을 잘 치기 위한 요령

준비

- 시험 한 주 전에 공부를 시작하라. 당신이 그 과목을 몇 번 본다면 시험 하루 전날 벼락치기하는 것보다 훨씬 더 많이 기억할 수 있을 것이다.
- 시험문제가 주로 어느 부분에서 나올 것인지, 어떤 문제들이 나올 것인지 선생님께 여쭈어 보라.
- 수업내용과 교재내용을 전체적으로 살펴 보고, 전체를 요약한 노트를 만들어라.
- 이해하지 못한 부분이 있으면 반드시 알고 넘어가라: 선생님께 물어보거나, 조교에게 물어보거나, 도서관에 가는 방법도 있다.
- 스터디 그룹을 만들어라, 다른 학생들이 놓친 부분들을 아는 학생들이 있을 것이다.
- 샘플 문제들을 만들어라. 수업내용을 생각하면서 나올 만한 문제들을 생각해 보라.
- 시험 전에 제때 식사하고 평소대로 적당한 수면을 취하라.
- 가능하면 아르바이트도 쉬고, 다른 활동들도 시험 후로 미루도록 하라.
- 어떤 수업의 경우(수학 같은 경우), 선생님께 기출문제를 요청해 보는 것도 괜찮을 수 있다.

에세이 시험의 준비

에세이의 경우, 충분한 근거와 함께 자신의 입장을 표현해야만 한다.

- 단순히 교재나 노트의 것을 재차 읽는 것 보다는 자신만의 생각들을 다시 언급하고 체계화하는 **연습을 하라.**
- 머릿속의 생각들을 자신의 언어로 표현하는 것을 **연습하라**. 시험 전에 그렇게 할 수 없다면, 아마 시험을 치는 그 순간에도 할 수 없을 것이다.

(… 페이지 2)

에세이 시험 치기

- 시험문제를 보기 전에, 유의사항을 꼼꼼히 읽어라.
- 그리고 전체 시험문제를 읽어보고 답할 수 있다고 확신이 드는 문제를 제일 먼저 선택하라.
- 각 문제들을 찬찬히 보면서, 무엇을 묻는지 정확히 판단하고, 키워드와 구절들은 밑줄을 그어라.
- 문제에 대해 생각하면서 원하는 중요한 정보를 기초로 간단한 초안을 작성하라.
- 에세이를 쓰기 전에 주제와 관련된 근거들을 고려하여 전체적인 골격을 만들어라.
- 문단을 새롭게 시작할 때는 명확한 주제문장과 함께 시작해야 한다는 것을 꼭 기억하라.
- 에세이는 반드시 질문에 대해 아주 직접적으로 다루어야 하고 그에 따른 구체적인 근거사실들을 제공해야 한다.
- 각 문제에 대해 반드시 무엇이라도 적어라. 비록 잘 모르더라도, 약간이라도 적는 것이 아예 안 적는 것 보다 낫다.
- 보기에 깨끗하고 깔끔하게 적어라. 채점하는 사람에게 좋은 인상을 줄 수 있다.

객관식 시험 치기

- 시작하기 전에 전체 문제를 읽어라. 확실히 아는 문제를 먼저 풀어라.
- 핵심 단어나 구절들은 밑줄을 그어라.
- 문제를 읽기 전에 답을 가려라. 머릿속으로 먼저 답을 말하고, 그리고 그 답과 가장 맞는 답을 선택하라.
- 답을 모르거나 불확실한 문제는 표시해두었다가 나중에 다시 풀어라.
- 오답 시 감점을 당하는 경우가 아니면 모든 문항에 답하라.

객관식 문제를 푸는 심화 전략

- 정답이 의심스러울 경우는 첫 번째 생각나는 것을 선택하라.
- 다른 문제나 답들로부터 나온 정보를 이용하라.
- 항상, 절대, 아무도, 모두 등이 포함된 문장은 정답이 아닌 경우가 많다.

(… 페이지 3)

DD 2003

- 명백히 정답이 아는 경우는 제거하라.

  예) 코

  a) 는 장배 형성 시기에 발전한다.
  b) ~~는 두 개의 움직이는 부분이 있다~~.
  c) 는 비개골에 의해 나누어져 있다.
  d) ~~는 균형을 잡는 기관이다~~.

언어 시험 준비

- 단어장을 작게, 연관이 있는 세트로 나누어라. 여러 번 반복하여 기억력을 향상시켜라.
- 당신이 일상에서 자주 접하는 문장들을 쓰면서 문법을 연습하라.

수학 및 과학 시험 준비

- 여러 공식들을 암기하라. 그래야 시험 시작과 동시에 적을 수 있다.
- 시험에 필요한 공식이나, 다이어그램, 사이클 등을 잘 복습해서 숙지하라.
- 교재에 굵은체나 이탤릭 체로 된 각종 용어의 뜻을 정의할 수 있어야 한다.
- 문제 푸는 것을 연습하라.
- 가능하다면 선생님으로부터 기출문제를 얻어라. 기출문제를 제한시간 내에 푸는 연습을 하라. 기출문제로 연습하는 것도 교재내용을 다루므로 훌륭한 준비가 된다.
- 작은 정보들이 전체 주제와 어떻게 연관되어 있는지를 이해하는 연습을 하라. 지식 체계에 대한 전반적인 이해가 없으면 서로 연결되지 못한 단편적인 지식만 기억하는 꼴이 된다.

[문장난이도 통계치: 단어 499; 단락당 문장 수 1.2, 문장당 단어 수 8.6; 수동태 0%, 문장난이도 88.1, 수준 3.1]

Dawson College Homepage - http://www.dawsoncollege.qc.ca/

DD 2003

TIPS FOR TAKING EXAMS

PREPARATIONS

- Begin studying a week before the exam. You will remember much more if you study several times than if you "cram" the night before.
- Ask your teacher what the exam will cover and what kinds of questions will be asked.
- Go through your class and textbook notes and make an outline based on both sets of notes.
- Clarify the material you don't understand: speak to your teacher, see a tutor, or visit the library.
- Form a study group: each student will know something that the others may have missed.
- Make up model questions; think of questions that bring together the course material.
- Eat on schedule and get a normal amount of sleep before the exam.
- If possible, take time off from your part-time job and suspend your other activities.
- In certain cases (such as math), you might ask the teacher to provide copies of previous exams.

PREPARING FOR ESSAY EXAMS

In essays you must express your position and support it with evidence, so:

- **Practice** organizing and restating ideas from the course rather than just rereading your text and notes. Think about how you would support or prove each point.
- **Practice** stating ideas in your own words. If you can't do so before the test, you probably won't be able to do so during the test.

TAKING ESSAY EXAMS

- Before looking at the questions, read the instructions *very carefully*.
- Then read all the questions, and select the ones that you are sure of to answer first.
- Examine each question, determining *exactly* what is being asked. Underline key words and phrases.
- Think about the question, and write brief notes based on the key information required.
- Before you write your essay, prepare a brief outline—your thesis and a list of supporting points.
- Remember the importance of opening each paragraph with a clear topic sentence.
- Make sure that your essay addresses the question *very directly* and provides specific supporting facts.
- Write *something* for every question. Even if you can't say much, something is better than nothing.
- Write clearly and neatly. This creates a more positive attitude in the person who is marking the exam.

TAKING MULTIPLE-CHOICE EXAMS

- Read all the questions before you begin. Answer the questions you are sure of first.
- Underline the key words and phrases in the questions.
- Cover up the answers before you read the question. Answer the question in your head, and then choose the response which best fits your answer.
- Mark questions which you cannot answer or are unsure of, and go back to them at the end.
- Never leave questions unanswered unless it is clear that incorrect answers count against you.

Further Strategies for Answering Multiple-Choice Questions

- When in doubt, go with your first guess.
- Use information from other questions and/or answers.
- Absolute words such as *always*, *never*, *none*, and *all* are often seen in false statements.
- Eliminate the answers that are clearly not correct

  Example: The nose

  a) develops during gastrulation

  b) ~~has two movable parts~~

  c) is structured in part by turbinals

  d) ~~is an organ of balance~~

PREPARING FOR LANGUAGE EXAMS

- Break vocabulary lists into small, related sets. Spread memorization out over several sessions.
- Practice grammar by writing sentences related to your own life.

PREPARING FOR MATH AND SCIENCE EXAMS

- Memorize the formulas, so that you can write them down as soon as the exam starts.
- Review formulas, diagrams, cycles, etc., which may be required on the test.
- Be able to define all terms that are in bold print or italics in your text.
- Practice doing problems.
- If possible, get copies of old exams from your teacher. Try writing them in the time limits set for the exam. Working with old exams also prepares you for doing problems out of the context of the textbook.
- Work toward understanding how all the bits of information relate to the whole topic. Without this framework for your knowledge, you are attempting to remember clusters of unconnected facts.

[Statistics: words 657; s/p 1.3, w/s 12.0; passives 6%, Reading ease 69.6, Grade level 6.4]

Dawson College Homepage - http://www.dawsoncollege.qc.ca/

DD 2003

EQUILIBRIUM

Or, The Keys To The Kingdom

Clear Thinking ↔ Readable Writing

A
B a s i c
C e n t r a l
D y n a m i c
E q u i l i b r i u m

Or, you could just imagine it as

널뛰기

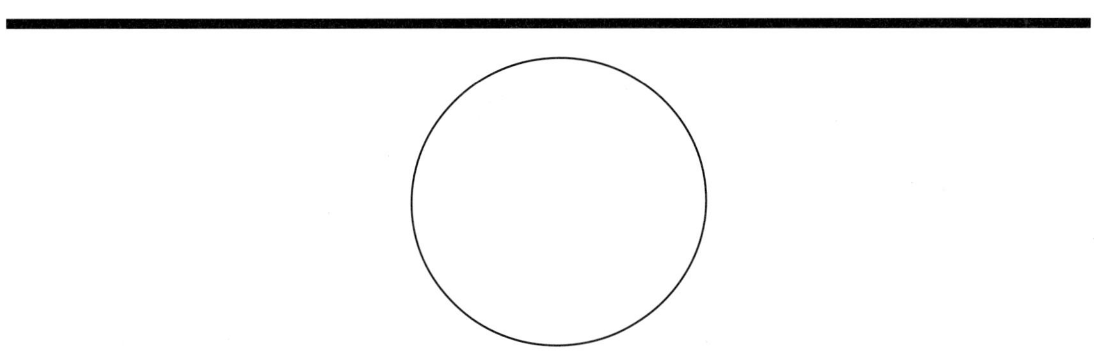

In Homage To Professor Rudolf Flesch
Writing Teacher Extraordinaire

Sept. 2008 © mns (V-21) *Technical Writing, An Introduction* *Michael Neil Shapiro*

PART 15 - Q & A

PART 1: Technical Writing, Definition & Description

이공계 영작문

쉬운 영어로 표현된 실무적 정의

이공계 영작문은 매뉴얼 사용자들에게 일을 수행할 수 있는 방법을 알려주는 글을 쓰기 위함이다.

성공적인 영작문

설명

성공적인 이공계 영작문은 읽는 사람이 잘 이해할 수 있는 형태로 정확한 정보를 제공함으로써 읽는 사람이 일을 잘 수행할 수 있도록 도와주어야 한다.

마이클 샤피로
정모교수역

Working Def'n, Descr'n (V-30) *Technical Writing, An Introduction* *2009.12.21 © mns*

Part 2: **Write Passive Sentences in ACTIVE (S-V-O) form**

1) Leonardo da Vinci painted The Mona Lisa.

____

2) France donated The Statue of Liberty to the United States.

____

3) A.G. Eiffel constructed The Eiffel Tower of iron beams.

Or, French people constructed The Eiffel Tower of iron beams.

____

4) Artists made the animated characters (out) of clay.

Or, Sculptors made the animated characters (out) of clay.

____

5) All the students completed this exercise very well.

____

Statistics: Words 74; s/p 1.0, w/s 9.2; passives 0%, Reading ease 55.5, Grade level 7.8

PART 9: Advanced Academic Writing – Medical Excerpt

Answers for Proofreading & Re-writing Exercise

Exercise A: Proofreading Instructions

1. Consider only the first paragraph on **Methods.**
2. Count the number of words 87-88 and sentences _1_.
3. What's the average number of words per sentence in paragraph one? 87-88.
4. What is the average number of words per sentence we try to achieve? _10_.
5. So, about how many sentences do we need, to tell all this information? _8_ or _9_.

Exercise B: Discuss and re-write the "Methods" section

1) Who is writing this article? Medical researchers; doctors; doctors doing research.

2) Why do people write research papers?

To get advanced degrees; to get money i.e. research funding / grants;
to communicate useful information. (How well did the writer succeed here?)

3) What word-processing tools did this writer FAIL to USE?

Didn't use Spelling & Grammar Check. Didn't use Readability Statistics, either!

3b) How do you know that? Typing error: "storke" is not a real word.
Sentence is 88 words long, and few can read it.

4) Three groups of people participated in this research. Name them.

- Medical researchers
- Stroke patients
- Control group of people in "normal" health

5) Why did people in each of these three groups come to the hospital?

- Medical researchers came to do research. Or, they usually work there.
- Stroke patients had a medical emergency. They had to come for help.
- Control group of people in "normal" health came in for routine health exams.

6) Write two sentences to describe each of the two patient groups.

The first group included 38 patients (male 18, female 20). They were admitted to the Dept. of Internal Medicine between August 2001 and June 2002, within 7 days after (apparently) suffering a stroke. Their diagnosis was acute cerebral infarction.

The second, or control group, was made up of 36 patients (male 17, female 19) who had described a normal state of health, without any history of stroke (including Transient Ischemic Stroke). They came in for routine health examinations from April to June 2002.

7) What is the key difference between these two groups?

The first group clearly suffered a medical emergency. The second group were "healthy".

8) Give this professional article an informative title.

A Comparative Study of Blood Static Patterns in Stroke Patients and Healthy Controls

Now, re-write the paragraph on Methods on the following page. One solution follows.

PART 9-B: Advanced Academic Writing Medical Paragraph Re-written

Here is an exact excerpt from an actual paper written for professional publication:

[TITLE?]

Methods : We compared the blood static pattern and symptoms according to The Diagnostic Criteria for Blood stasis Syndrome between patient group 38 patients(male 18, female 20) that admitted due to acute cerebral infarction within 7days after stroke attack in Dept. of Internal Medicine, [City] Oriental Medicine Hospital from August 2001 to June 2002 and control group, 36 patients(male 17, female 19) that had described normal state without a history of storke(included Transient Ischemic Stroke) through the health examination from April 2002 to June 2002.

Statistics: Words 87, sentences 1; s/p 1.0, w/s 87.0; passives 0%, Reading ease 0.0, Grade level 40.8

◙ Can you see that the writer could have caught and fixed many errors by using **spell check?** The Spelling and Grammar Check Tool also points out the long sentence. Can you see where the statistics tell us that this writing is unreadable? **(Reading ease 0.0 and Grade level 40.8.)**

♀ ♥ ♂

Here is one possible re-writing of the same section of this medical research report:

A Comparative Study of Blood Static Patterns in Stroke Patients and Healthy Controls

Methods: In this study, we compared the health records of two groups of people. All were patients examined at the [City] Oriental Medicine Hospital between August 2001 and June 2002.

Specifically, we compared patients' blood static pattern and symptoms, according to The Diagnostic Criteria for Blood Stasis Syndrome.[1]

The first group comprised[2] 38 patients (male 18, female 20) that[3] were admitted to the Dept. of Internal Medicine (August 2001 to June 2002) due to acute cerebral infarction, within 7 days after suffering a stroke.

The second, or control group comprised 36 patients (male 17, female 19) who had described a normal state of health, without any history of stroke (including Transient Ischemic Stroke), during routine health examinations (April - June 2002).

Statistics: Words 120, sentences 5; s/p 1.2, w/s 24.0; passives 0%, Reading ease 26.6, Grade level 15.5

Stats (incl. title): Words 133; sent. 5; s/p 1.2, w/s 24.0; passives 0%, Reading ease 26.6, Grade level 15.5

---

[1] *[Where, and by whom, is this set of criteria published/accepted?]*
[2] Included, comprehended *(active verbs)*; ***or,*** was composed of, was made up of *(passive verbs).*
[3] It is preferable to refer to persons as "who" rather than "that", although "that" is acceptable.

PART 10: Q & A, Engineers Without Borders – V.O.A. Report

Class # ______ Student # 2001XXXX Name *Hong Gil Dong* Date ________

Instructions—Listen, read, then fill in the blanks:

1. Who started this organization, and when? A civil engineering professor, Bernard Amadei launched the group in the year two thousand (*or,* 2000).

2. What university did that professor and his students belong to? *(Para. 3)* They belonged to the University of Colorado at Boulder.

3. How many projects does the group have currently? (# # #) They have about three hundred (300) projects in forty-five (45) countries.

4. What kind of organization is "Engineers Without Borders"? *(See para. 4.)* It's an international, nonprofit organization.

5. What did they do in Nepal, and why? *(See paragraph 5.)* They set up a sun-powered computer to communicate with a school in Kathmandu.

6. Very briefly, what have volunteers built in a) Guatemala and b) Kenya?
   a. They have built ten bridges for isolated communities;
   b. They have built windmills to improve crop production. *(See para. 6)*

7. Cathy Leslie is the executive director.

8. The group has eight thousand members, including students. They hope that more than 10% will be non-engineers.

9. What other kinds of professional help do villages need? *(Paragraph 8)* They need help to develop business plans, and ways to finance and supervise projects.

10. Local chapters usually work with communities for five to ten years.

Statistics: Words 217; s/p 2.0, w/s 8.6; passives 0%, Reading Ease 53.4, Grade Level 7.9

Engineers w/o Borders Q & A *Technical Writing, An Introduction* *2009.11.02 © mns*

PART 10-B: Powered Flight – Answers

V.O.A. Wright Brothers

Velocity (Speed)

1) 37m / 12 = 3.08 m/s
2) 260 / 59 = 4.40 m/s
3) Increase = 4.40 – 3.08 = 1.32m/s. As a percentage of initial velocity, 1.32 / 3.08 = 42.857 = 42.9%

Duration (Time)

4) The longest flight lasted 59 seconds; the first flight lasted 12 seconds. So, the longest flight was about five times (5X) as long as the first.

5) 1903 duration ≈ 1 minute; 1908 duration = 1 hour. This is 60 times (60X) as long. Expressed as a percent, the increase in flight time was 60 X 100 = 6000 %.

Statistics: Words 93; s/p 2.0, w/s 10.0, passives 0 %; Reading Ease 59.6, Grade Level 6.8

Powered Flight Q & A *Technical Writing, An Introduction* *2009.6 © mns*

PART 11-A: Electric Kettle Booklet

Questions & Answers

1. What **kind** of booklet is this?

   Answer: It's an **"Instruction manual".** (See the subtitle, *if you can!)*

   You could also call it an **"Owner's Manual"** or a **"User's Manual".**

2. Which page is not normally **numbered**?

   Answer: The **front cover** is not normally given a **printed** number.

   (But it still counts as a page!)

3. What is/are the biggest **problem(s)** you find in reading this manual?

   Answer: a) The size of the letters (font) is much too small.

   b) The letters are too faint. The print is not clear and black.

4. **Before using** the kettle for making hot drinks, **what** should the owner **do**? (pg. 2)

   Answer: i) Fill the kettle with clean water.

   ii) Boil the water.

   iii) Empty the kettle.

   iv) Repeat this procedure 5-6 times.

5. What does CE **mean**? Why is it **printed** on the manual for this electric kettle?

   Answer: a) It means, "This product complies with all essential rules applicable to it."

   OR, It means, ***Conformité Européesne***; or in English, **"European Conformity".**

   Answer: b) It is printed on the manual because

   - the manufacturer wants to sell the product in the European Union.

   OR,

   - it is a **mark** required by the European Union.

Technically, or **officially, according to EU law,** this is called "CE Marking".

(See the CE Marking page of this section, and the Internet for more detailed info.)

Score _____/ 10

Statistics (V-9): words 232; s/p 1.2, w/s 8.7; Passives 12%, FRE 73.9, GL 5.0

PART 11-B: Electric Shaver Booklet: Questions & Answers

Philishave 600 Series by Philips

1. **How many pages** of instructions are in this booklet? Answer: Eight (8) (1)

2. **Instructions are available** in Thirteen (13) languages. (1)

3. **List, in order,** the eleven main section headings (in the black bars): Important (1)

   Charge indications, Charging, Shaving, Trimming,

   Cleaning, Replacing the shaving heads, Storing,

   Disposal of the battery, Troubleshooting, Guarantee & service

4. **List three (3) features** [of many] that make this manual easy to read, understand and use.

   - Font is big enough to read comfortably.
   - Black bars divide contents into sections
   - Pictures and drawings help us to find and understand the information. (1)

5. **Can I clean** this electric shaver using running water? YES / NO (Circle your answer.) (1)

6. How do I know when the battery is fully charged? (To answer, write a sentence.) *[See note.]*

   The green **led** (or, indicator light) will start blinking. (1)

*[**Note**: It's NOT a "pilot" light. Gas-powered boilers have those. It's a light-emitting diode, or led.]*

7. **Can I shave** with the power cord plugged in? YES / NO (Circle your answer.) (1)

8. **How long** will this electric razor (or shaver) work on battery power after it's fully charged?*

   It will work for about 30 minutes after it's fully charged. (1)

9. **Thinking Qn:** List two factors that can affect how long the razor works on one charge. (2)

   ►Newer batteries hold their charge better than old batteries.

   ►The thickness of the beard, or toughness of individual hairs, will change the "load", or

demand on the battery power. *[See next page for additional ideas & answers.]* Total _____/10

* **Discuss the difference** between "approximately" (about) *[= + / -]* and "up to" *[= max. or limit].*

Stats (V-2): words 284; s/p 3.2, w/s 9.5; Readability: passives 0%, Reading ease 68.1, Grade Level 6.1

Shaver Ex. Q & A *Technical Writing, An Introduction* *2009.11 (2008) © mns*

PART 11-C: Electric Shaver Manual

More Answers to Questions Four (4) & Nine (9)

4. List features that make this manual easy to read, understand and use.

- Instructions are available in thirteen (13) languages.
- The font is big enough to read comfortably.
- Good vertical spacing between lines of writing.
- Black bars divide content into 11 sections.
- Many items are numbered.
- White numbers in black boxes are easy to read.
- Concise, short sentences.
- Negative instructions are usually underlined.
- Pictures and drawings help us to find information and to understand that information.
- This manual shows A/S information in section eleven (11). (10)

9. Factors that may affect how long the razor works on one full battery charge.

- Extreme cold or heat may affect how well the battery holds its charge.
- Old batteries don't hold their charge as well as new ones.
- Charging a battery after it is completely discharged allows maximum stored charge.
- Battery power used during shaving depends on how thick the beard hair is and how tough the individual hairs (whiskers) are. (4)

Stats (V-6): words 174; s/p 1.1, w/s 9.8; Readability: passives 6%, Reading ease 61.3, Grade Level 7.1

PART 13: Answers on "Writing Is A Technology" Assignment

Find the Key points

Instructions:

A. You may do this assignment alone, or with a partner.

B. Write a **list of key points** that you find in this essay. Use the numbers (1 to 8) below.

HINT: DO NOT read the whole essay. Just find the key points. Then write them down.

C. Where's the **best place to look** for this information? (Answer in a short sentence.)

The best place to look could be at the beginning, in the Abstract, or at the end, in the Discussion or Conclusions.

***Hints for C**--key information and where to find it: This **list of key points** can also be called an **abstract** or a **summary**. The name depends on the position. An abstract appears in advance; a summary usually follows the article.

[Memory device: **A**bstract in **A**dvance, **S**ummary follow**S**.]

D. Give this list a good, clear **title**. Put your title on the line, above point #1. Center it.

[Hint: What is this list?] ***Don't make it hard! Make it clear and simple.***

List of Key Points from "Writing Is A Technology"

1. Writing is a major human technology.

2. It is the memory of the human race.

3. It is an evolving technology.

4. Koreans have historically been leaders in developing such technologies.

5. We can and should benefit from the best writing technology available.

6. Writing technologies depend upon standard protocols

7. Our first task is to master standard writing protocols.

8. Then we will apply our knowledge to specific writing tasks.

Answer Page Statistics (V-18): Words 259; s/p 1.6, w/s 8.8; passives 3%, FRE 75.2, GL 4.8

WIAT, Find Key Points *Technical Writing, An Introduction* *2009.02.17 © mns*

COURSE REVIEW QUESTIONS

Technical Writing, An Introduction

20 NOVEMBER 2008

JOB APPLICATIONS (5 points)

Based on your high quality resume and cover letter, an excellent company has invited you to come for an interview, ASAP. Congratulations! Now, what did you do well in your application package? List five items. Write one sentence for each.

-
-
-
-
-

MANUALS (5 points)

Your company plans to sell its new product in Europe. Your team is assigned the job of writing the instruction manual. List five (5) important things you should include in it.

-
-
-
-
-

EDITING ACADEMIC WRITING (5 points)

A member of your research team has written a report of your work. He asks you to proofread and edit the document. He gives you a print-out on paper, and an electronic version in MS-Word. What will you do next? Write your action plan as a five-point list.

-
-
-
-
-

DEFINITIONS

Write a clear, short definition for a **Rule of Thumb**. (2 points)

-

Write one good definition of **Proofreading**. (3 points)

•

Based on this course, write a definition of **Technical Writing**. (5 points)

•

CHANGING PASSIVE TO ACTIVE SENTENCES

Rewrite the following sentences in active form. Remember to put the people back in.

• The Eiffel Tower was built of iron beams. (2 points)

•

• All the characters in *Wallace and Gromit* were originally made of clay. (3 points)

•

COURSE GOALS (3 points)

List the three **student goals** we learned on Day 1 of this course. Write in <u>sentences</u>.

•

•

•

RESEARCH REPORT (5 points)

We edited part of a medical research report. What made that writing so hard to read?

•

TOEIC *Beside the point!* (Or, 2 points)

Write one (humorous?) description of T.O.E.I.C.

GENERAL (What was the key point for you?)

What is/are the most useful thing(s) you learned in this Technical Writing course?

•

•

•

Stats (V-9): Words 292, s/p 3.1, w/s 8.6; passives 7%, Reading Ease 75.1, Grade Level 4.9

Photo Credits—Covers
Technical Writing, An Introduction
***BILINGUAL* (E-K) Edition**

Front Cover:

Buljo jikji simche yojeol, UNESCO/Jikji Memory of the World Prize, *http://portal.unesco.org*

Back Cover:

Top: T-50, Lockheed Martin, published on *Scientific Frontline website: www.sflorg.com/aviation*

Lower Left: Geobukseon, *www.tabula-rasa.info/JamesAdams/treasure_trove/koreanTurtle/korean_ts.htm*

Lower Right: Seungnyemun, Korean National Heritage Online, *www.heritage.go.kr/eng/nat/nat_01.jsp*